The Spatial Dynamics
of Modernization
in Sierra Leone

The Spatial Dynamics of Modernization in Sierra Leone:

STRUCTURE, DIFFUSION, AND RESPONSE

J. Barry Riddell

Northwestern University Press

Evanston   1970

J. Barry Riddell is Assistant Professor of Geography
at Queen's University, Kingston, Ontario.

Table of Contents

List of Tables

List of Figures

Preface

The process of change in Africa is a variegated phenomenon. The attitudes, behavior patterns, and inner desires of a few people have changed dramatically; for many they have begun to be modified and restructured; yet for most, life remains much the same today as it was over a century ago. In the cities new ideas are taking hold and new ways of life are emerging; hints of these changes diffuse outward along the railways and roads and through the small hinterland towns; but in isolated areas the impulse has yet to be strongly felt. On the national political stage there is often turmoil and struggle as new systems evolve to replace the European models left as legacies of the colonial past; however, at the same time the old, autocratic chiefdom system still operates over much of the countryside.

These changes, be they economic, political, social, or psychological, all reflect the process of modernization—the striving toward something new, a unique blend of Western prototypes and African dreams. Many academic disciplines have been and are studying the modernization process, each focusing upon its own separate subject matter and methods of inquiry; seldom are the approaches and findings effectively integrated. Yet modernization does have a common underlying dimension—a spatial or areal expression. It is a spatial-diffusion process, moving outward across the land as it spreads along the transportation network and through the emerging system of urban places.

This monograph considers the geography of modernization in Sierra Leone, treating it as a process of spatial diffusion, operating within a spatial fabric defined not only by the frictional effects of distance but also by the network of road and rail and the hierarchy of city, town, and village. In addition, the spatial implications of the process are shown to be reflected in the emerging pattern of urban migration, and movement is described in terms of a descriptive linear model.

The research upon which this study is based was carried out in Sierra Leone during 1967 and in the archival sources in London during the winter of 1968. The study was made under a fellowship granted by the Foreign Area Fellowship Program. However, the conclusions, opinions, and other statements in this publication are those of the author and not necessarily those of the Fellowship Program.

To Fourah Bay College, Sierra Leone, and especially to the Institute of African Studies and to Dr. Milton Harvey, Lecturer in Geography, I extend my sincere appreciation for making my stay in Sierra Leone productive and exciting. Many officials of the Departments of Works, Health, Railway, Co-operation, Interior, Education, Posts and Telecommunications, and of the Central Statistics Office of the Government of Sierra Leone lent generous support to my project, answering the many questions and providing much of the detail.

The librarians of the British Museum, the Public Records Office, the Commonwealth Office, the Institute of Commonwealth Studies, and the Royal Commonwealth Society, London, and of Fourah Bay College, Freetown, were most helpful in procuring old and obscure documents and reports.

I owe a special debt of gratitude to Professor Allan Rodgers and to the staff and graduate students of the Department of Geography of The Pennsylvania State University for advice, encouragement, support, and above all, a stimulating environment.

The Graduate School of The Pennsylvania State University generously provided a fellowship for two years during the writer's residence. Similarly, an academic term in the Program of African Studies at Northwestern University provided stimulus in interdisciplinary African study.

Two people deserve special mention. Professor Peter Gould has advised, encouraged, and given so much of his time and enthusiasm. My wife Dona helped in so many ways that this work is dedicated to her and to the country we both came to love.

J. BARRY RIDDELL

The Spatial Dynamics
of Modernization
in Sierra Leone

Introduction: Sierra Leone

All this tumult of enterprise and exploration and high unfashionable ideals and death—what has it left behind that matters? Ports, railways and roads. A respect, a hunger for education. An ideal that justice should be independent. A dissatisfaction upon which new and better societies could be built. The apparatus of a Civil Service and a hospital service—though only in skeletal condition.[1]

Much has been written of the colonial situation, of its origins, its history, its imprint on the map, and its impact upon the minds of men. Although it has been characterized as many things, it was essentially a period of modernization, a time in which the ideas, methods, and techniques of European society were imposed upon or melded into traditional ways of life. In Africa, it brought dramatic and often painful changes. Yet at the same time, Western medicine was slowly introduced; missionaries brought European forms of education, as well as Christian theology; the European administrators imposed peace and security; and the roads and rails they built brought commerical and other secular values, and occasionally prosperity.

This study considers one aspect of the colonial situation within one national setting—the geographic patterns of change in Sierra Leone in the period since the 1896 declaration extended a British protectorate over the hinterland. Thus it develops a geography of Sierra Leone, although a very specialized human geography, focusing on the spatial dimensions of change. Three dominant and tightly interwoven themes characterize the areal pattern of change and development. First, a modern network of road and rail was imposed upon a simple, indigenous system of bush paths and riverine routes. Second, along the new lines of communication and among the growing urban places, modern facilities—post offices, banks, hospitals, and schools—diffused. Finally, and in response to such structural and institutional alterations, new patterns of population movement emerged, dominated by the growing urban foci.

Founded in 1787 as a small settlement of freed slaves, Sierra Leone became a British crown colony in 1808 and gradually grew in size as thousands of

1. P. O'Donovan, "When the Empire Closed Down," *The Observer* (London), January 21, 1968, p. 2.

3

men and women were landed from the slave ships liberated by the British navy. With the declaration of the protectorate over the hinterland in 1896, the former small, peninsular colony expanded to almost one hundred times its previous size. The new area was virtually devoid of any form of modern structure, as the lasting effects of previous contact had been minimal. Small amounts of trade moved inland to and from the coastal ports; missionaries penetrated the rivers to establish churches and schools; traders, and previously slavers, established a few coastal and riverine posts; and a few colony Creoles conducted business inland.[2] But the impact of these earlier contacts was small and localized, and was virtually wiped out by the Hut Tax War, which almost immediately followed the British declaration.

Upon the restoration of order, the railway was extended across the southern half of the country and the diffusion of modernization began. Feeder roads were built from the rail line to tap the potential of adjacent areas; commercial firms established trading facilities at the junction points; and the money economy, with all its connotations for social and cultural change, spread along the growing transport system. At the same time, the Christian missions re-established posts along the river routes and began to spread their influence along the railway and up the roads. Rudimentary public health services were established at the district headquarters, and postal services and banking facilities were extended upcountry.

Not surprisingly, the evolution of the transport network has been largely dependent upon the initial location of the railway. Once the line was built, a very large investment was fixed in both the economic and spatial senses, and most decisions relating to network growth, other than those determined by administrative priorities, depended upon it. Until World War II, expansion from the initial line of penetration was largely a matter of extending the rail hinterland by the construction of feeder roads. Consideration was given in the late 1920's to the idea of an independent road network, and some attempt was made to link the individual

2. A. Howard, "The Role of Freetown in the Commercial Life of Sierra Leone," in *Freetown: A Symposium,* ed. C. Fyfe and E. Jones (Freetown: Sierra Leone University Press, 1968), pp. 38–64.

pieces of feeder road into a system. However, such an idea was never carried through, and road transportation never achieved an independent and competitive ability. It was only the accident of the Second World War which led to the gradual evolution of a road network independent of the rail system. A road link was forged inland from Freetown to connect with the protectorate system as an alternative route in case the railway was sabotaged. Gradually the route was improved and a national network of roads extended, with the result that the railway lost much of its economic *raison d'être*. The final stage of this process has been the announcement in the 1967 budget speech of the gradual closing of the railway and plans for the concomitant improvement and expansion of the road net.

The process of network growth was never independent of other forms of modernization. Sometimes it was the leading directional force, other times only a reflection. For example, early postal services expanded laterally along the coast and inland up the railway route. Gradually they extended from these axes via river routes or feeder roads, but later the need to extend such services to isolated administrative centers led to further network expansion.

The expansion of educational opportunities also illustrates the directional force of transportation, at least in the early years. Mission activity expanded educational facilities into the protectorate from the early nineteenth century. The first mission stations were coastal, later moving inland up the river routes. With the building of the railway, mission schools opened along the line and later along the feeder roads. Since World War II the interstices have begun to fill in and new influences have emerged, but the imprint of transportation can still be seen on a map of schools.

For some services, the strong influence of the developing transport network was modified by administrative requirements and decisions. The provision of health services illustrates such an effect, because of the policy of locating health facilities first at district headquarters, then later in the larger towns. The influence of the transportation network on this pattern can still be seen, however, for the largest towns were usually the first to receive health facilities, and to some degree, size was a function of position within the road and rail system. Since independence in 1961, the government has pursued a policy providing for an areal hierarchy of health facilities with a hospital in each district headquarters, health centers in several of the larger towns, and at least one dispensary or treatment center in each chiefdom.

While many modern services and facilities have filtered down the emerging urban hierarchy and through the growing transport network, some have been much less influenced by such structures. The co-operative movement is a classical example of the areal diffusion of a contagious institution through areas of greater or lesser receptivity, depending upon local economic and geographic conditions. Proximity or access to the spreading idea is the dominant factor, although tribal differences and administrative decisions are significant in determining the pattern during certain periods.

Whether spread through the network or by hierarchical or contagious processes of diffusion, the new services and facilities greatly modified local conditions. New ideas and values spread along the roads and through the educational system. Traditional society often began to appear repressive and dull. Money to buy the new luxuries could be earned by new forms of labor, or by employing the new skills learned in the local school. People began to widen their areal horizons as the limits of the world began to expand beyond the village, section, or chiefdom. New opportunities were perceived in the mines and towns. A new life was possible; one only had to move to it.

And movement began, but not as before. It grew to a size never before seen, and the emergence of urban foci provided an entirely new orientation. The provincial towns attracted the local people, offering urban environments still within the geographic and social sphere of the traditional society. Then gradually, as the urban transition was made and people acquired new skills and attitudes, the hold of the local area weakened. Later, perhaps in the next generation, migrants moved on to the larger, more exciting towns with greater opportunities in the distant parts of the country—many proceeding to Freetown, the administrative and economic capital.

This very general description, a series of geographical vignettes, outlines the major themes of transport network growth, the diffusion of modernization, and the migration of people in response to such evolution. Each of these themes is tightly interlocked, and the interwoven processes take place against a very specific geographical background, molded by the colonial situation and dominated by the oppressive difficulties of a tropical environment.

THE SETTING

The name Sierra Leone derives either from the leonine shape of the mountains of the colony peninsula when viewed from the sea, or from the thunderous storms, typical of the onset of the tropical rainy season, as they break over the mountains. Yet the coastal range from which the country derives its name is hardly typical of the generally flat and monotonous nature of the interior plain. It is only the occasional inselberg and the rougher plateau lands to the north and east that deviate from the low, level surface of the land. Well over half the area lies below 500 feet, and only a few peaks exceed 3,000 feet.[3]

Climatically, Sierra Leone is typical of West Africa, being continuously hot and having heavy precipitation with a very marked seasonal periodicity. Because of the orientation of the coastline and the resultant steady onshore southwesterly winds of the high-sun season, rainfall exceeds 200 inches on parts of the colony peninsula and averages over 100 inches per year for the country as a whole. Mean daily temperatures are approximately 80° F. throughout the year, although the rainy season is somewhat cooler. Diurnal ranges exceed annual amplitudes.[4]

Because of the heavy rainfall and its marked periodicity, the drainage network is exceedingly dense. Historically, this was an advantage because the sys-

3. G. J. Williams, "A Relative Relief Map of Sierra Leone," *Sierra Leone Geographical Journal,* XI (1967), 11–14. Also, J. I. Clarke, *Sierra Leone in Maps* (London: University of London Press, 1966), contains an excellent series of maps depicting the physical base.

4. S. Gregory, *Rainfall over Sierra Leone* (University of Liverpool, Department of Geography, Research Paper No. 2, 1965).

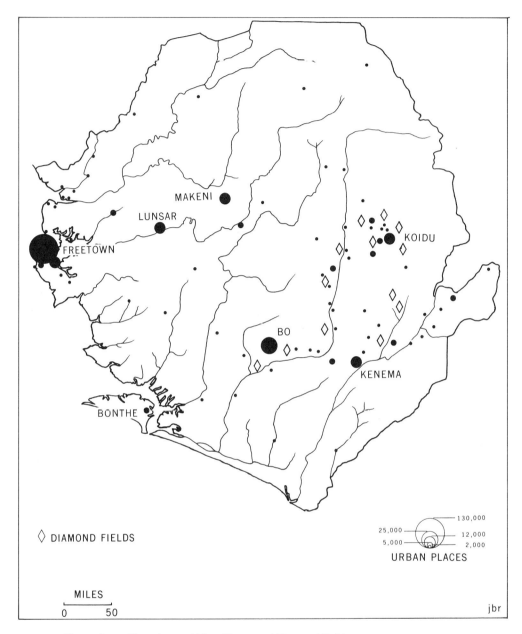

Figure 1.   Sierra Leone: Urban Places and Diamond Fields

tem of streams and rivers provided a ready, if very rough, transport system ori-
ented in the general direction of trade (Figure 1). Today, however, with the expansion of the modern transport system of rail and road, high stream densities
frequently mean higher bridging and construction costs, while periodic
flooding disrupts traffic flow by rendering ferries inoperative or by washing out
bridges.

Although broad-scale vegetation maps of Africa depict much, if not all, of Sierra Leone as tropical forest, the actual pattern has been greatly distorted by agricultural activity. The result is that primary forests are only found in a few, more remote reserves. With population densities averaging 78 persons per square mile and exceeding 100 in many areas, almost all the land is cropped under a shifting bush-fallow system, so that the dominant forms are bush farm and grassland.[5]

The history of Sierra Leone prior to the British proclamation of a protectorate over the hinterland is the story of the settlement of freed slaves at Freetown and the gradual emergence of the Creole society in the peninsular crown colony.[6] Official British interest in the hinterland, except where it influenced the activities of the trading firms, was one of relative indifference. Even as late as 1865, Parliament considered dropping all British "obligations" in West Africa with the exception of the small Sierra Leone colony.[7]

However, in the late nineteenth century, relations with the interior became steadily stronger. Prior contacts had often been in the form of punitive expeditions against warring chiefs in order to protect the colony from attack and to maintain peaceful conditions for inland trade. As the tempo of the "Scramble for Africa" increased and the French penetrated to the north and east, a British sphere was gradually delimited on the map and legitimized with the 1896 declaration.

Culturally, Sierra Leone is distinctly plural, and even after over seventy years the former colony and protectorate are still well defined, not only in terms of contrasting Creole and tribal histories and societies but also in terms of land holding, local government, ethnic mix, and urbanization. The tribal chiefdoms of the interior originally numbered over 200 units, although by the process of amalgama-

5. The survey of Sierra Leone's physical base is brief, partly because of its limited relevance to the analysis which follows, but also because of the well-annotated set of maps to be found in Clarke, *Sierra Leone in Maps*.

6. C. Fyfe, *A History of Sierra Leone* (London: Oxford University Press, 1962); C. Fyfe, *Sierra Leone Inheritance* (London: Oxford University Press, 1964); A. T. Porter, *Creoledom* (London: Oxford University Press, 1963).

7. K. Little, *The Mende of Sierra Leone* (London: Routledge & Kegan Paul, 1967), p. 43, cites a recommendation of a parliamentary committee of that year.

tion the number has been reduced to the present 146. These territorial units, averaging between 100 and 200 square miles in size, are largely separate from one another, each under the personal rule of a supreme chief. At another level, however, there are forms of co-operation and association among the chiefdoms, and among many there is a feeling of affinity, especially in areas such as Mende or Temne country where one tribal group predominates. At the same time that outside contact brought closer unity among the peoples of the protectorate through trade, transport, and urban growth, it also brought about basic religious divisions within the country, not only among the several competing Christian missions but more especially between the nominally Christian southern half of the country and the Muslim north.

The economy of Sierra Leone is a complex amalgam of traditional and market economies. Based upon a largely communal land system, the vast majority of the population is engaged in traditional subsistence agriculture, employing primitive tools for working small plots. Because of the harsh environmental conditions, new fields are cleared every five to ten years. Rice is the principal food crop, and, although the less productive upland varieties predominate, increasingly large areas, both on the coast and inland, are being devoted to swamp varieties. Cassava, yams, and maize provide secondary dietary supplements.

Despite the prevalence of subsistence forms of agriculture, the economic history of the country has been dominated by the production of crops for export to the European market. Through the last half of the nineteenth century and as late as the 1930's, trade consisted largely of palm kernels, though significant volumes of kola, ginger, and rubber were also exported. The railway location, in fact, was largely determined by the location of the richest palm country in the far southeastern sector of the country.

Since 1935 mineral exports have exceeded agricultural, although significant quantities of piassava began to be exported from the Pujehun and Bonthe Districts from the 1930's, and by the 1950's coffee and cocoa had become important exports (Table 1). The development of minerals has been revolutionary. The Marampa iron mine, opened in 1935, has drawn workers from all over the coun-

TABLE 1.   Annual Export Income (in millions of pounds sterling)

Year	Total Export Income	Palm Kernels	Iron Ore	Diamonds	Other
1920	2.25	1.40	—	—	0.85
1930	1.05	0.67	—	—	0.38
1940	2.12	0.38	0.54	0.78	0.42
1950	6.66	2.28	1.28	1.56	1.54
1960	25.93	2.93	4.14	16.48	2.38
1964	30.44	2.44	5.22	19.91	2.87

SOURCE: O. P. Bagai, "A Statistical Study of the Exports of Sierra Leone, 1920–64," mimeo. (Freetown: University College of Sierra Leone, n.d.).

try, and although its profits have been largely diverted overseas it has had a marked impact on the development of a wage-labor class. Chromite was mined for a brief time at Hangha and the new rutile and bauxite mines appear promising for the near future. Since the early 1950's, diamonds have been the major source of export revenue. The Kono fields and the alluvial diamonds of the Sewa River have drawn men from all parts of the country and beyond. Although great wealth has been attained by a few, and the government has been provided with its largest single source of income, civil disruptions and lawlessness have caused severe social and political difficulties in Kono, and there have been marked reductions in the production of rice and other food staples.[8]

8. H. L. van der Laan, *The Sierra Leone Diamonds: An Economic Study Covering the Years 1952–1961* (London: Oxford University Press, 1965).

Structure: The Growth of the Administrative System and the Transportation Network

Only those who have felt the isolation and the almost menacing atmosphere of the forests of Tropical Africa can realise just what a symbol of freedom and progress is presented by a road.[1]

The habitat . . . is the city. Here is the centre of commerce, the seat of government, the source of news and innovation and the point of contact with the outside world.[2]

The complex process of change, which has been variously termed development, growth, and modernization, is the outcome of the complex interaction of several forces. Although changes in each of the economic, social, political, demographic, and psychological elements are necessary, it is the provision of a transportation infrastructure and the concomitant easing of movement as well as the focusing of economic activity and human organization in new urban centers which are the most decisive factors. Without roads and rail, produce rots on the trees or in the fields for lack of accessible markets; without towns and cities there are no foci for new ways of life to emerge. Ideas and innovations spread only very slowly in the absence of roads and towns, if at all, and the provision of services and the administration of government are made difficult, if not impossible. It is the transport network and the urban hierarchy which bind together the disparate regions of the country; it is along the railway and roads and through the towns that the money economy with all its developmental implications spreads. The road and the town, as they evolve, indicate change and a new life.

THE EVOLUTION OF THE ADMINISTRATIVE SYSTEM

The growth of the system of urban places in Sierra Leone reflects the evolution of the colonial administrative organization and the beginnings of trade and com-

1. Great Britain, Colonial Office, *Report by the Hon. W. G. A. Ormsby-Gore, M.P. (Parliamentary Under-Secretary of State for the Colonies), on His Visit to West Africa during the Year 1926*, p. 30.
    2. H. Miner, "The City and Modernization: An Introduction," in *The City in Modern Africa* (London: Pall Mall Press; New York: Praeger, 1967), p. 1.

merce along the transport system. Thus the urbanization process has had two driving forces—the administrative, with its bundle of social and economic services, and the commercial. The spatial arrangement of urban places induced by the two forces were at least partially similar. Administration involved the provision of certain services in a hierarchical arrangement over geographic area; trade resulted in the growth of towns at the break-of-bulk points and key junctions in the transport system as well as the several centers in the mining areas. At times the two forces were interacting and identical in their areal pattern, and administrative and commercial functions were often found in the same towns.[3]

The Areal Organization of Colonial Administration

Together with the transportation system, the areal administrative hierarchy effectively defines the very fabric of the country with which the vectors of change are most strongly associated. The transport and communications networks were structured, at least partially, with reference to the district and provincial capitals; it was within the headquarters towns that many of the modern institutions and services were located; and it was from these centers that policies were implemented and information spread. The system of administrative regions and headquarters was not constant throughout time but was periodically redefined as administrative objectives were re-evaluated and as geographic space was continuously restructured and refocused by the evolving transport and communications networks.

With the declaration of the protectorate in 1896, the former major interior police posts at Karene, Panguma, Bandajuma, and Falaba, as well as the village of Kwellu, were designated as the district headquarters to administer the five districts of Karene, Panguma, Bandajuma, Koinadugu, and Ronietta, respectively

3. There are many obvious exceptions to the above generalization; however, the following analysis will emphasize the administrative system, as it was a major vector through which modernization spread. A much broader study of the evolution of urban centers in Sierra Leone is in M. E. E. Harvey, "A Geographical Study of the Pattern, Processes and Consequences of Urban Growth in Sierra Leone in the Twentieth Century" (Ph.D. diss., University of Durham, 1966).

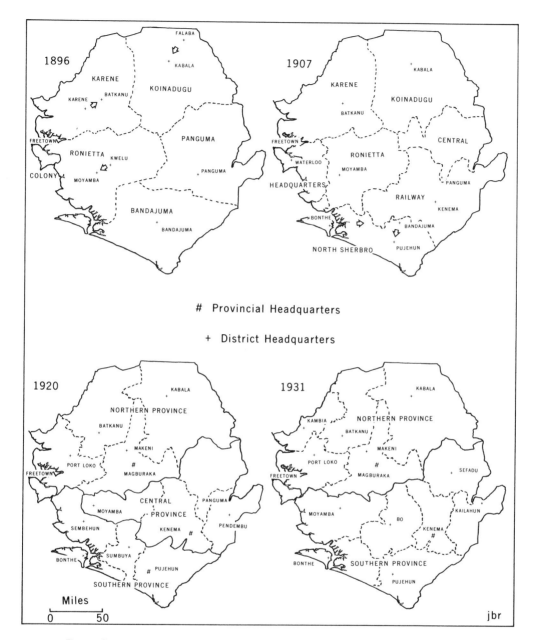

Figure 2.   Administrative Regions, 1896 to 1931

NOTE: Arrows indicate changes in the location of headquarters.

(Figure 2). These centers served as the seats of administrative authority, and district officers and their staffs were attached to each. In 1901 several of the headquarters were moved to new locations (from Falaba to Kabala, from Karene to Batkanu, and from Kwellu to Moyamba) to take advantage of better sites; but the district boundaries remained essentially unaltered.

With the opening of the railway and the construction of a series of feeder roads, changes in the political organization of the protectorate became necessary by 1907.[4] The area served by the easternmost extension of the line was included in the Panguma and Bandajuma Districts (Figure 2). However, it was considered that those chiefdoms through which the line ran, and in which new roads were being constructed, should be brought under the administration of one district commissioner. Thus the Panguma and Bandajuma Districts were amalgamated into a new Railway District, and Kenema on the rail line was chosen as the headquarters. The northern part of the old Panguma District, as well as parts of the adjacent districts, were combined to form the new Central District until it was dissolved in 1909 and incorporated within the Railway District. The southern chiefdoms of the old Bandajuma District, as well as several from the Ronietta District, were incorporated into a new North Sherbro District administered from Bonthe. The western part of the Ronietta District was also separated as the new Headquarters District, administered from Waterloo. Karene and Koinadugu remained essentially intact. The pattern remained unaltered until 1920, though several subdistricts were created in the Railway, Karene, and North Sherbro Districts, and the headquarters of the North Sherbro District was shifted to Bandajuma in 1911 and to Pujehun in 1913.

By 1919 it had become apparent that, despite the 1907 alterations, the administrative system was not yet in accordance with the geographic realities of the protectorate. The colonial officials' mental image of the area they administered became clearer as more information was gained through experience and as geographic space was restructured by transportation improvements. The opening of the northern branch line of the railway provided a vital communications link into the northern interior, while the river systems attained renewed importance as connecting threads into both the northeastern and southeastern corners of the country. The administrative system was realtered by Ordinance No. 4 of 1920;[5]

4. Great Britain, Colonial Office, *Colonial Report, 1906, Sierra Leone.*
5. Governor Wilkinson to Colonial Office, September 25, 1919, "Protectorate Administration."

the five districts were dissolved, and in their stead, three new provinces, each with four districts, were created (Figure 2). Once again the new provinces essentially reflected the transportation system in effect at the time. The Central Province included the areas served by the railway, the Southern Province the Sherbro waterways, and the Northern Province the branch line of the railway and the Rokelle and Scarcies river systems. Provincial headquarters were established at Magburaka (Northern), Kenema (Central), and Pujehun (Southern), and district headquarters were located in the larger or more accessible towns. With but minor alterations, the system continued until 1930. In a search for administrative optimality, and to adjust to changing accessibilities and to correct mistakes of the partitioning, a few alterations were made. In 1922 a short-lived Mano River District was created from the eastern part of the Pujehun District; the Kambia and Ronietta Districts were added to the Northern Province in 1927; the headquarters of the Kono District was shifted to Sefadu; and a new Panguma District was created.

In January, 1931, as a result of the constantly changing geographic conditions, the protectorate administrative system was again reorganized (Figure 2). The programs of motor-road construction of the late 1920's made possible the amalgamation of the Southern and Central Provinces by making overland travel less difficult and thus administration more efficient. In effect, the area which could be administered by one commissioner was expanded. The number of districts was reduced from ten to seven in the Southern Province. No changes were made in the Northern Province, where the districts had been comparatively large and where new road construction had not altered routes to the same extent as in the south.[6]

The system, with but a few minor alterations,[7] remained intact until January, 1940, when the administrative organization reverted to the old district and

6. Sierra Leone, *Sessional Paper* No. 4, 1930, *Administrative Sub-Divisions of the Colony and of the Protectorate.*

7. The headquarters of the Northern Province was moved to Freetown from Magburaka in 1932, the Kambia District was dissolved in 1935, Karene was dissolved in 1934 and re-established in 1935, and Tonkolili District with headquarters at Mabonto was created in 1936 from parts of the Koinadugu and Bombali Districts.

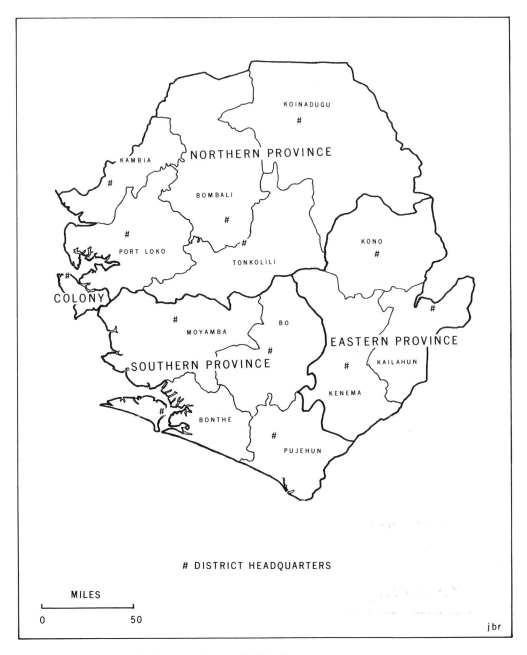

KOINADUGU
#

NORTHERN PROVINCE

KAMBIA
#

BOMBALI
#

PORT LOKO
#

KONO
#

TONKOLILI
#

COLONY
#

MOYAMBA
#

BO

EASTERN PROVINCE
#

SOUTHERN PROVINCE
#

KAILAHUN

KENEMA

BONTHE
#

PUJEHUN
#

DISTRICT HEADQUARTERS

MILES
|_____|
0   50

jbr

Figure 3.   Administrative Regions, 1946 to Present

subdistrict system for the duration of the war.[8] In 1946 the three-province system was reborn and has continued essentially unchanged to the present (Figure 3).[9]

        8. Sierra Leone, *Sessional Paper* No. 5, 1939, *Correspondence Relating to the Reorganization of Protectorate Administration.*
        9. Sierra Leone, *Sessional Paper* No. 7, 1945, *Administrative Reorganization of the Pro-*

With the provision of new and expanded developmental funds under the 1946 de-velopment plan and the revised Colonial Development and Welfare Act, a new tier was added to the system to oversee the program. Bo was created as the protectorate headquarters, a senior commissioner was appointed, and rep-resentatives of the various government departments were stationed in the town to assist and implement the District Development Plans. Bo emerged as the focal point of the protectorate and the link to Freetown was strengthened with the construction of a more direct road and trunk telephone service. Since independence, the two-tier system has been reapplied, and Freetown has continued as the dominant focus of provincial administration, while Kenema (Eastern), Bo (Southern), and Makeni (Northern) continue as the provincial headquarters.

Throughout its history, administrative redistricting has been dominated by alterations made in the transport and communications networks of the country. Administration is a service provided from more or less central positions to sur-rounding areas. Thus, as accessibility patterns change over time, areal centrality is altered and, in order to keep the administrative system as efficient as possible, adjustments must be made.[10] Thus the transport network, as it evolved, caused a restructuring of administrative areas, and at the same time transport growth was partly in response to administrative needs.

TRANSPORT NETWORK GROWTH

As it grew, the transport system of Sierra Leone restructured and refocused geo-graphic space. It provided a framework upon which the administrative system was built, hints of change spread, and goods and people began to move. It defined a

---

tectorate; the only alteration was the dissolution of the Karene District in 1949 for the sake of effi-ciency.

10. Occasionally ethnic factors were vital, as was the case in the creation of the Kono District in the area settled by the Kono peoples. In addition, the basic areal units, the chiefdoms, created an ethnic base.

structure within which a system of urban nodes began to emerge in response to administrative complexities and the evolution of an exchange economy.

Prior to 1896 there were no improved forms of transportation. Rather, natural networks were employed—the open sea, the riverine routes, and the overland bush paths. The frictional effects of distance upon movement were naturally immense, for even the waterways were subject to periodic floods and frequent rapids and shallows. Overland movement was disturbed by the convulsions of intertribal conflict. Despite these problems, goods and people did move over great distances, and the hinterlands of the coastal ports, such as Freetown and Bonthe, extended well beyond the present national boundaries.[11] However, the trade was low in volume, often irregular, and was limited, except over short distances, to high-value goods such as gold and ivory. Wheeled traffic was nonexistent; goods were head-loaded, and officials and dignitaries were carried along the bush paths by suspended hammock.

In 1895 a transportation revolution had begun with the construction of a railroad from Freetown. The idea of a rail line extending the British sphere inland from the Sierra Leone colony dates to the report of Blyden's goodwill expedition to the king of Falaba in 1872, in which he suggested a link from Freetown to the present northeastern corner of the country.[12] In 1888 the first formal construction proposal was made by a European trader in Freetown, who suggested establishing a private company to construct a line northeast from Freetown for 140 miles, later to be extended to Timbuktu. Several reasons, including pressure from the Creole community,[13] and the fact that the scheme involved a

11. Discussion of trade patterns prior to the 1896 declaration of the protectorate may be found in Governor F. Cardew, *Railway Schemes for the Colony of Sierra Leone* (address presented to the Liverpool Chamber of Commerce, August 1, 1895; published in pamphlet form by the African Trade Section of the Incorporated Chamber of Commerce of Liverpool, August, 1895).

12. E. W. Blyden, *Report on the Falaba Expedition, 1872* (Freetown: Government Printer, 1872).

13. S. Lewis, "Minutes of the Legislative Council, May 5, 1895," quoted in *Sierra Leone Inheritance,* ed. C. Fyfe (London: Oxford University Press, 1964), pp. 258–60.

government guarantee of the investment,[14] have been suggested for the Legislative Council's rejection of the plan. However, the major cause of its demise was probably a simple lack of interest on the part of the Colonial Office at the time.

By 1890 conditions had changed. Popular pressure was so intense in Sierra Leone that local legislative support for the venture was inevitable.[15] With the French penetration in Guinea, the views of the Colonial Office had altered and a railway was seen as an effective means of establishing British sovereignty inland, as well as providing an administrative tool and an economic arm of the trading firms. The Liverpool and Manchester Chambers of Commerce pressed for the line,[16] and the West Africa Empire Limited Company published a scheme to extend a line from Freetown as far inland as the Niger River.[17]

As the original location and orientation of the railway proved to be so decisive a factor in the evolution of the entire transportation system, the locational decision was, and continues to be, of prime importance. Prior to 1895, all discussions of the railway examined a route extending northeast from Freetown. In effect, the rail would tap the same areas served by the riverine routes which provided Freetown's major trade arteries at the time.[18] However, Governor Cardew's extensive tour of the protectorate effectively redefined the perceived economic space of the hinterland.[19] In the far southeastern corner of the country, in what is now the Eastern Province, Cardew found vast areas rich in the palm products so much in demand in Europe for glycerin and margarine. He reasoned that

14. J. R. Best, "A History of the Sierra Leone Railway, 1899–1949," mimeo. (Freetown, 1949), p. 5.

15. *Ibid.*

16. R. J. Church, "The Railways of West Africa—A Geographical and Historical Analysis" (Ph.D. diss., University of London, 1943), pp. 92–93.

17. Best, "History of the Sierra Leone Railway."

18. Refer to the maps in P. K. Mitchell, "Trade Routes of the Early Sierra Leone Protectorate," *Sierra Leone Studies,* XVI (1962), 204–17.

19. See Cardew, *Railway Schemes.* An excellent account of the expedition is also given in T. J. Alldridge, *The Sherbro and Its Hinterland* (London: Macmillan, 1901); Alldridge was a district officer who accompanied Cardew on the tour.

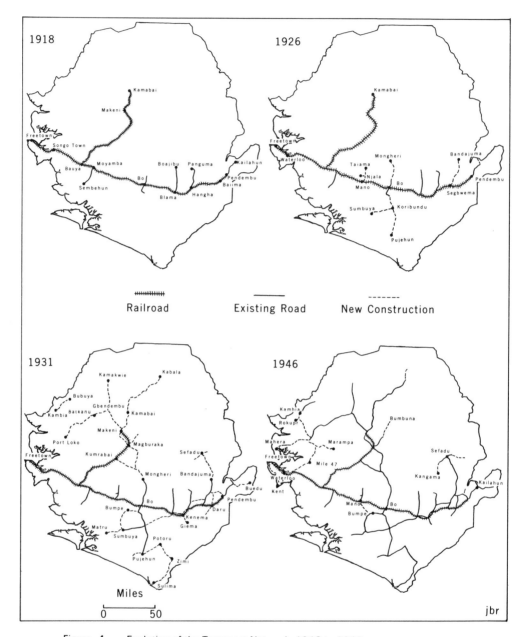

Figure 4.   Evolution of the Transport Network, 1918 to 1946

an extension southeast would open these areas to trade with Freetown, and that such a route would be economically more viable than the extension to the relatively less productive savannah country to the north.

Thus, in 1895 the colony began construction of the railway. The Hut Tax War of 1898 interrupted the early building, but it also provided proof of the effectiveness of the line in moving troops. By 1899 the railway had reached

TABLE 2.   TOTAL EXPORT REVENUE,
1896–1912

Year	Value of Exports, £ sterling
1896	449,033
1898	290,991
1900	362,741
1902	403,518
1904	484,870
1906	716,623
1908	736,755
1910	1,249,367
1912	1,540,754

SOURCE: Great Britain, Colonial Office,
Colonial Reports, 1896–1912.

Songo Town, the furthest extension of the colony, and by 1904 had been extended to Baiima, 220 miles from the terminus and deep within the palm-rich Upper Mende country (Figure 4). The gauge was narrow because of the lack of capital, pessimistic expectations, and military fears which required a width different from the French lines. Because of terrain difficulties, and due to the lack of a prior survey, the route was circuitous and tortuous. Nevertheless, it had an immediate impact, as produce was shipped from all along its route, although it was not until Blama (Mile 169) was reached and the palm country tapped that any large quantities were generated. The intervening area only provided a modicum of exportable produce.

Export trade increased markedly, especially in palm kernels. From 1901 to 1903 the average annual value[20] of palm kernels exported was £186,000 sterling, but from 1905 to 1908 it increased to £344,000 (Table 2).[21] Unfortunately, it soon

20. Tonnage shipped would perhaps provide a more meaningful measure of impact, but the figures are not available. However, the increase in value does index a strong increase in volume of exports.

21. Great Britain, Colonial Office, *Colonial Report, 1908, Sierra Leone,* p. 5.

became apparent that the impact of the line was limited to a few miles on either side. In 1904 Governor Probyn wrote to the Colonial Office:

> Until proper roads are made however the oil (Palm Oil) can only be brought to the railway as a head load in kerosene tins, etc., and it is obvious that as long as this is the case the oil will only be collected from places in the near vicinity of the railway. . . . I have consulted those who best know the country and the new conditions of trade brought about by the expansion of the railway and there is a consensus of opinion that until good roads are made the benefits of the Railway will be relatively small and that the natives, unless aided, would not greatly improve the roads for many years.[22]

With the completion of the main line, the governor announced a scheme or making roads from certain points on the line to act as feeders for produce from the interior. The Railway Surveyor was transferred to the post of Superintendent of Roads in the protectorate, and by 1905 a program of feeder-road construction had begun. Though they were only improved bush paths, some permanent bridges were constructed, and as a result of such demonstrations, roads were also built by several of the protectorate chiefs.

By the close of 1906, 59 miles of "first-class" roads had been constructed and declared by the governor as improved roads,[23] and a further 120 miles had been upgraded. Consideration was also given to improved means of transport on the new roads. Experiments were made in the use of animal power, traction engines, and barrel-roller transport, and in the following year, tram lines were extended from Baiima and Boia.[24] As soon as the work of the Roads Department took effect, the impact was apparent. Traders established shops along the roads, large European firms and many Syrian traders built factories at the junction points with the rail line, and the export of produce was greatly expanded.[25] The

22. Governor Probyn to Colonial Office, November 11, 1904, "Scheme for Inaugurating a Roads Department and Road Construction."

23. *Sierra Leone Gazette,* July 30, 1906.

24. Governor Probyn to Colonial Office, July 12, 1906.

25. Governor Probyn to Colonial Office, July 1, 1905; Governor Probyn to Colonial Office, January 25, 1906.

impact upon the administrative system has been discussed.[26]

The feeder roads had a marked impact not only on the volume of traffic, but especially on the growth of urban places at the junction of road and rail. Here, classic break-of-bulk economies occurred and European, Syrian, and Creole firms established factories to buy produce and sell imported goods. The earliest were set up at Bo, Blama, Hangha, and Segbwema, and later branches extended to Pendembu, Kenema, Mano, and Moyamba. The sequence of events at Bo was typical and illustrative. The railhead reached Bo in January of 1903, but no trading firms arrived until 1906, when the new feeder road connected the town to a rich palm area to the north.

> . . . with the result that many traders as well as two of the European firms established stores there, and by thus creating a market at which the natives could sell produce for good prices, caused them to desert an ancient trade route which, crossing the line at a point 10 miles nearer to Freetown than Bo, led to Sumbuya, a trading station in touch with Bonthe.[27]

Although no data on town size are available for the time period, it is clear that a new line of towns grew up at the junction points and challenged the traditional coastal and riverine ports and larger chiefs' towns for numerical and economic importance.

By 1911 the impact of the railway was still quite limited. While export crops moved from the rail hinterland in considerable volume, the areal extent of the impulse was severely confined. The experiments using animal power and motorized carriers had failed, and with the exception of barrel-rolling in a few local areas, the new roads served largely as improved bush paths for head-porterage. For these reasons it was decided to halt road construction until motorized trucks came into use in the protectorate.[28] The Roads Department continued, but only as a maintenance crew. Energies were redirected to the railroad,

26. See above, pp. 14–19.
27. Great Britain, Colonial Office, *Colonial Report, 1908, Sierra Leone*, p. 6.
28. Governor Merewether to Colonial Office, April 3, 1912.

and the tram lines which extended for short distances from Baiima and Boia were incorporated into the system. The returns from the Boia branch were so encouraging that within five years the line was extended 104 miles to the northeast through a rich palm belt and beyond into the savannah country.

The appearance in 1916 of the first commercial truck in the protectorate brought back the optimistic atmosphere of the early rail-construction days.[29] The roads were narrow, discontinuous, and lacked bridges at several important points, but the fact that trucks ran on them meant that constant pressure was applied to improve and link them together (Figure 4).

Although several of the feeder roads had been lengthened by the early 1920's and many miles of road projected or constructed as nonmotorable tracks, the network remained a series of short, disconnected feeders. Despite the fact that trucks had been in use since 1916, few were in evidence, their impact was slight, and head-porterage and barrel-rollers remained the dominant forms of transporting goods. The system, as it existed, did not provide an adequate basis for the economical use of motorized transport. The Commissioner of the Central Province wrote in 1922:

> I consider this to be due to the fact that at present these roads are unsuitable for lorries of more than one ton load, and the cost of carrying produce on one-ton lorries is said to be in the neighborhood of one shilling per ton-mile, thus rendering their employment unprofitable.[30]

In effect, the nature of the roads was limiting the use of motor vehicles and the limited use of motor vehicles was acting as a brake to further investment in roads.[31] Although the Colonial Report of 1922 lists 291 miles of roads, in fact only

29. The first truck was employed by a Syrian trader at Bo (see Governor Wilkinson to Colonial Office, February 22, 1917), though almost immediately another owned by a Creole trader appeared on the Blama-Boajibu road.

30. Sierra Leone, *Annual Report of the Central Province for the Year 1922*, p. 11.

31. Of the motorable roads in use at the end of 1922, only the Moyamba-Sembehun (3), the Blama-Boajibu (6), the Hangha-Panguma (1), and the Pendembu-Kailahun (1) had commercial trucks plying their length; thus there were only 11 trucks in the entire protectorate (*ibid.*).

120 miles of these were permanently bridged and the longest motorable stretch was 24 miles (Blama-Boajibu). The statement of the governor of Sierra Leone to the Private Enterprise Committee in the London Parliament in 1923 aptly summarizes the situation:

> Motor roads in Sierra Leone are certainly few and short compared, say, with the Gold Coast, but here again there is singularly little demand for more roads, or for road extensions, from the commercial community. It must be remembered that our chief produce—palm kernels—is a commodity which cannot stand heavy transport charges; and as the only roads that Sierra Leone can afford are such as will only carry light lorries it follows that the cost of a motor journey can only be spread over a small volume of produce. Hence the cost of motor transport, for any except short journeys, is high and responsible merchants have informed me that 20 to 25 miles is the economic limit for motor transport in Sierra Leone.[32]

Thus, during the early years of the century the rail line was constructed and its hinterland was areally expanded by the construction of a series of feeder roads. In no sense was the system efficient or economic, yet its effects over a limited area had been dramatic, expanding the hinterland of Freetown far into the interior, leading to the growth of a line of new towns and providing the stimulus for an expanded production of crops for sale. The network remained like a tree; the main trunk was extended and a few short branches were extended, but its areal coverage was limited.

The Emergence of the Road Network

By the mid 1920's, however, a combination of circumstances led to a marked increase in road construction. First, the financial position of both the government and the traders had improved from the slight depression of the early 1920's. The government, in fact, was in the unusual position in 1925 of having a surplus of

32. Great Britain, Parliament, *Minutes of the Private Enterprise Committee, 1923* (C.O. 766–1).

funds remaining from the budgets of 1924 and 1925,[33] and a portion of the money was set aside for the expansion of the road network. For the first time, roads were thought of as other than feeders to the railway, and though the Mongheri-Kumrabai, Kamabai-Kabala, and Bandajuma-Sefadu roads were extensions of feeders, their primary purpose was to open new areas to trade and to assist in the administration of the country. A further road was built to link a cocoa-producing area to the sea in the far south of the country.

At the same time, the government's decision to expand the road network was strongly reinforced by the visit and subsequent report of Mr. Ormsby-Gore, parliamentary undersecretary of state for the colonies. He was shocked by the feeble transport system of Sierra Leone, composed of the railway and only six short feeder roads, and by the almost universal use of head-porterage. He compared conditions in Sierra Leone to those of the other West African colonies and emphasized the importance of transport facilities to administration, commerce, and the general livelihood of the peoples. He re-emphasized the fact that motor traffic would not develop unless the roads were lengthened and connected. Roads were to be the key to African development:

> Apart altogether from the supreme importance of roads as the first essential in developing modern and more economical means of transport, the civilising influence of a road is a paramount consideration. Without roads you will not get the itinerant trader and the village shopkeeper, who play such a large part in creating new wants and stimulating production, to provide the purchasing power for these wants. The road more than anything else tends to break down the narrowness and the circumscribed life of the African native.[34]

The comments had importance not so much for their substance as for their impact. The report was read and acted upon in London as well as in the capitals of

33. Sierra Leone, *Sessional Paper* No. 15, 1925, *Despatches Relating to the Surplus Balances Development Programme, 1925.*
34. Great Britain, Colonial Office, *Report by the Hon. W. G. A. Ormsby-Gore.*

West Africa.[35] In the five-year period from 1926 to 1931 the network of motorable roads expanded from 224 to over 800 miles. Five sessional papers outlining plans to expand the road network further appeared within two years of the visit.[36] The network suddenly grew from a series of short, disconnected feeders to one providing a thin areal coverage over much of the map. Most important perhaps to the future economy of Sierra Leone was that many were built without reference to the rail line and some even in direct competition with it.

The early planning of the expansion was largely the responsibility of one man—the governor. He was advised by his administrative officers and cajoled by pressure groups such as the Creole community and the European Chamber of Commerce, but the final decision, aside from the Colonial Office, was his prerogative. Only in a few cases did roads originate through local initiative, and these were built because local chiefs had undertaken the clearing and stumping and the government later brought them to motorable standards. Up to 1928 planning was not formalized and construction was largely based upon individual road projects. These roads partially linked the network together, extended the system of feeder roads, or linked producing areas to navigable stretches of water. The only formal set of goals seems to have derived from the general remarks of Ormsby-Gore.

The planning process was radically revised in September, 1928, when a Central Roads Board was formed to examine the requirements of the protectorate and prepare a program of road construction for the following three years.[37] The board consisted of colonial administrative officials and gave no voice to local interests, although the European Chamber of Commerce was represented. They outlined a program for 150 miles of government roads and 150 miles of chiefs' roads. The plan included the linking of all the existing roads in the protectorate, extending several new feeders, and explicitly specified roads to be built to open new areas to development.

35. See also the governor's address to the Legislative Council, Freetown, following the visit (Sierra Leone, *Legislative Council Debates, Session 1926–1927*).

36. Sierra Leone, *Sessional Papers* No. 5, 1927; No. 9, 1927; No. 3, 1928; No. 4, 1928; No. 6, 1928.

37. Governor Byrne to Colonial Office, October 3, 1928.

Most noticeable was the enlarged role to be played by the chiefs and peoples of the protectorate in building new roads. Half were to be built by local efforts. Interest in road construction had previously been quite limited and confined to a few areas. However, about this time a marked change in local attitudes toward road-building appeared:

> There has been a great change in the last three years in the attitudes of chiefs and people of this province towards motor-roads. Until the Koribundu-Pujehun and Koribundu-Sumbuya roads were being freely used (1925 onwards), the people had little interest in motor-roads and in parts a positive dislike to them. Now they see rice prices kept stable, head porterage disappearing, speed and comparative comfort in travel, they are everywhere clamouring to be allowed to make such roads for themselves.[38]

Sweeping changes occurred over the next few years (Figure 4). New areas were opened to trade, the efficiency of administration in areas away from the railway increased, and the country began to be tied together by the system of roads and rail. Above all, the series of short feeders had been extended to a much more expansive connected network.

Many years were to pass before Sierra Leone could reap the benefits of this expansion. The 1930's were years of depression, and the export economy suffered unforeseen losses. The difficult financial situation meant that road construction was halted and that only minimal funds were provided for maintenance. One road was abandoned (Kambia-Bubuya), and the only new roads were the few short stretches or improvements by the mining companies or from monies arising specifically for local development from the Mining Benefits Fund scheme.

During its entire history, the railway had not shown a profit or even been able to match revenues to expenditures. In fact, in 1929 the mountain line, serving the Freetown suburbs, was closed, and the following year the Makeni-Kamabai section of the branch line was torn up and converted to roadway. Given the rail-

38. Sierra Leone, *Annual Report for the Provincial Administration for the Year 1928*, p. 19.

TABLE 3.   BLAMA AND MAKENI RAIL SHIPMENTS (TONS)

	Total Tonnage Shipped			Palm Kernels Shipped	
Year	Blama	Makeni	Year	Blama	Makeni
1924	7166	3068	1925	5510	2950
1928	6875	2491	1929	4633	1447
1929	6162	2018	1930	3441	1434
1930	4655	1917	1931	4144	1811

SOURCE: Annual reports of the Railway Department.

way's precarious financial position and the added hardships of the depression years, the effects of the new road construction of the late 1920's began to be felt severely. The Port Loko–Makeni and Blama-Koribundu-Sumbuya roads operated directly as competitors to the railway, providing road links to the riverine ports from areas formerly served exclusively by the line. Even in the planning stage such adverse effects on the rail traffic had been noted, but such detrimental possibilities were offset by the fact that the roads served to link disparate parts of the system (Blama-Koribundu-Sumbuya) and administrative headquarters (Port Loko–Batkanu–Makeni). The impact was sharp and shipments of palm kernels and imported goods were especially curtailed (Table 3). In noting the sharp decline in kernels shipped from Makeni, the district commissioner wrote:

> The fall is so great that the ordinary reason of trade depression fails to account for it and I cannot help feeling that the opening of the motor road from Port Loko to Batkanu is largely responsible by enabling traders to establish at Batkanu and there to purchase palm kernels that otherwise would have been purchased at Makeni. . . . The difference in freight from Makeni to Freetown by railway and from Batkanu to Freetown by lorry and water enables one pound per ton more to be paid at Batkanu than at Makeni. There is no exact means of checking the volume of trade at Port Loko but it is significant that there are now two European firms established there where formerly there were none and that the Syrian population has also increased and now numbers some seventy persons. . . . When the remaining portion of the road between Makeni and Batkanu is finished in

1930, giving free access between Makeni and Port Loko, and so by water to Freetown, considerable impetus will be given to use of motor transport for carrying
goods. . . . Port Loko is already increasing its trade at the expense of Makeni
and history is thus repeating itself in a curious way. Up to about 1910 before the
building of the northerly portion of the branch line the bulk of the Northern
Province produce and general trade went to Port Loko which suffered severely
when the railway was opened for traffic. It would appear that the opening of
motor roads will again restore lost traffic to Port Loko and render it more important than it has latterly been. In this connection may be noted the fact that
whereas a few years ago there were no motor-launches at Port Loko there are
now no less than nine.[39]

Similar effects were felt at Blama by 1930, and 2,745 tons were diverted to the
road with a loss to the railroad of £28,450, largely made up of higher-value
imports.[40]

An ordinance to authorize the levying of tolls on highways in the protectorate was put to the Legislative Council and passed in 1932.[41] However, the governor considered it to be premature and unpopular both to the mercantile community and to the chiefs and people of the protectorate who gave their labor freely to
the construction of the roads.[42] In addition, the ferry crossing fees on the Port
Loko road severely reduced the impact of the road at the time. With the elimination of the tolls after the government took over operation and maintenance of the
protectorate ferries from the United Africa Company in 1935, the problem arose
again. As a result, the 1932 ordinance was implemented, and from January, 1935,
a toll of £2 was levied on all vehicles carrying imported goods toward Makeni.[43]

Despite the toll, the railway continued to lose traffic to the road and river

39. Sierra Leone, *Annual Report of the Provincial Administration for the Year 1929,* pp.
3–4.
40. Summarized from proceedings of the Conference on Railway Revenue and Expenditure in Sierra Leone, 1931.
41. Ordinance No. 16, 1932; the Legislative Council debates of the time contain
interesting discussions of the problem of road and rail competition.
42. Despatch, June 29, 1932.
43. *Sierra Leone Gazette,* January 17, 1935.

routes, and a railway observer on duty at the toll gates on the Port Loko–Makeni road estimated that the railway lost traffic valued at just over £3,000 during 1935 (representing 5 per cent of railway revenue).[44] Again in 1936 a further ordinance to regulate the carriage of goods by road was put to the Legislative Council and passed as Ordinance No. 6 of 1937.[45] It effectively eliminated motor competition with the railway by imposing duties on road transport. Later it was also applied to a section of the newly constructed Mano-Bumpe road.

With the lifting of the depression, the need for restrictions and tolls disappeared and another period of road construction began. For the first time Freetown and the protectorate were linked by road when a route was extended from Waterloo to Port Loko, and Colonial Development funds were employed in opening a circular road around the colony peninsula, thus linking the isolated villages with the capital. The Second World War brought further restrictions to construction once again, although two important links were started, one extending north from Port Loko to Kambia and the other (later to become the country's main road) from Mile 47 on the Freetown–Waterloo–Port Loko road to Kumrabai Mamilla (and thence to Bo and beyond by the existing road). The latter was begun by the army as an alternative to the rail system in case of sabotage.

The Postwar Period

The postwar period was a time of exciting plans and frustrating disappointments. In 1943 a Development and Planning Officer was appointed to prepare a plan of economic development, which was to begin with the termination of the war, taking advantage of the monies available under the new Colonial Development and Welfare Act. The plan called for improvements in communications, fuller exploitation of natural resources, and an expansion of welfare services. It also predicted marked improvements in economic standards and general health.[46] However, the

44. Best, "History of the Sierra Leone Railway," p. 84.
45. *Sierra Leone Gazette,* July 29, 1937.
46. Sierra Leone, *An Outline of the Ten-Year Plan for the Development of Sierra Leone* (Freetown, 1946).

plan proved to be no plan at all, but rather a listing of aims and ideas. There was no blueprint for implementation. "The designers of the 1946 Plan gave no specific indication of the magnitude of the desired change or how such changes, even had they been specified, were to be effected."[47] Equally as restricting was the fact that the technical and supervisory staffs, so necessary to implement the schemes, were simply not available.[48]

The transport plans included the construction of 290 miles of new roads in the protectorate. The general purposes of the roads were:

1. to insure that all Government centres and other important towns are on the trunk road system,
2. to open up areas hitherto untouched, and
3. to open roads to the French Frontier and to connect with the French road system.[49]

The plans also provided for the replacement of 10 ferries in the protectorate by major bridges. However, the road plans were never specified, and the first bridge was not completed until 1955. Most of the available plant and staff were used on the Mile 47–Kumrabai road, as the shortened link assumed first priority with the establishment of Bo as the administrative headquarters of the protectorate. The pace was slow, and by 1949 a new, more specific, detailed plan was prepared.

The Childs Plan examined the entire transport system and made specific proposals to expand and restructure the network.[50] For the first time, the road system was considered as an entity in itself, operating in large part independently of the railway. Childs even posed the question of closing the line:

The possibility of turning over to roads even at this stage was considered but found impractical. The position is governed by the existence of the railway, in which

47. R. G. Saylor, "The Economic System of Sierra Leone, with Special Reference to the Role of Government" (Ph.D. diss., Duke University, 1966), p. 285.

48. Sierra Leone, *Progress Report on the Development Programme* (Annual Reports, 1946–51).

49. Sierra Leone, *Ten-Year Plan,* p. 13.

50. Sierra Leone, *A Plan of Economic Development for Sierra Leone* (Freetown, 1949).

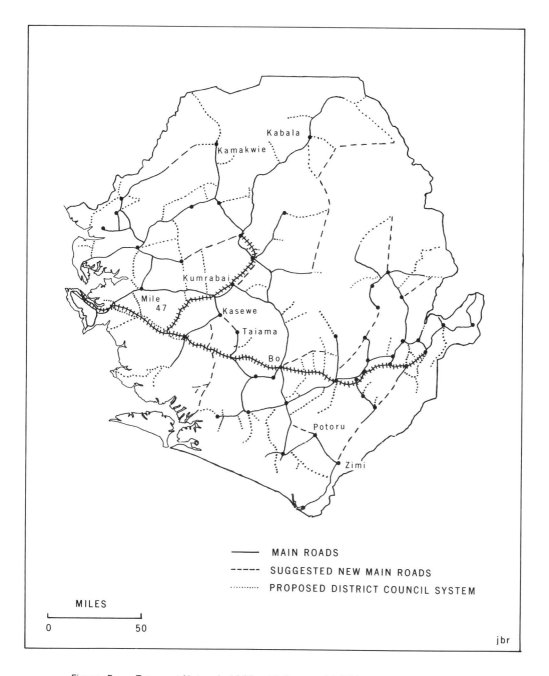

Figure 5.   Transport Network, 1949, with Proposed Additions

considerable capital has been sunk, the present absence of roads of adequate cal-
ibre to take the place of the railway, and the uncertain prospect of obtaining either
the staff or equipment to build them.[51]

51. *Ibid.*, p. 29.

The provincial roads program was to direct as much traffic as possible to the railway, but roads not having this effect were not excluded (Figure 5).

A specific five-year road-construction program was outlined, and a Roads Board was established to determine priorities and to continuously re-evaluate the program over a period of time. The bases of the network improvement were to be the major link from Freetown into the protectorate and the increase of efficiency of the over-all system by replacing the ferry crossings with major bridges. All the roads opened new areas and several of them became important links in the protectorate system. The Taiama-Kasewe link was vital in reducing the distances to Bo and beyond, providing for the first time a ferry-free route into the heart of the protectorate.

There was complaint that the publication of the Childs Plan put undue pressure on the government, and especially the Public Works Department, to show immediate, visible results:

> Great efforts were made nevertheless to produce something which the public could see. This, of necessity, meant many ad hoc decisions which, in more normal times, would not have been made without much further investigation, information and plans. In other words the officers concerned continually took what has been described . . . as "Colonial Risk"—a fact not realized by people outside the Department.[52]

In a sense this was true. Basic information, such as traffic density, traffic desire, population distribution, and areal production figures were not available. However, unlike their predecessors, they did have a rather detailed plan based upon the best information available, and the Roads Board continued to rethink and re-evaluate the road-construction program for a period of two-and-a-half years.

Perhaps most essential were the local area developments. The District Councils had existed since 1945 as advisory committees; now they were converted to local development planning and executing agencies. All 12 District Councils drew up plans of local development, and although they were limited in scope and

52. Sierra Leone, Director of Public Works, *1951 Report, Public Works Department.*

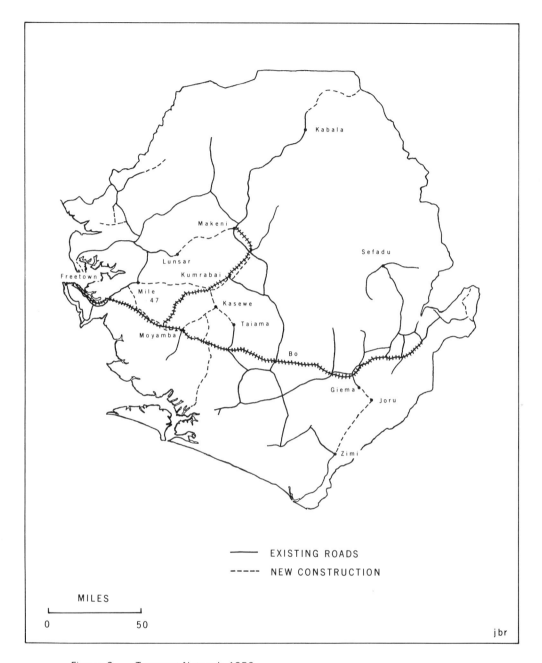

Figure 6.   Transport Network, 1956

financial support, they did make local leaders think about planning on a scale
larger than the local village or chiefdom for the first time.[53] Roads were built at
the district level, and though they were often short and of poor quality, they were

53. D. M. Hedges, "Progress of Kambia District Council, Sierra Leone," *Journal of
African Administration*, V (1953), 30–34.

TABLE 4.   TRAFFIC CENSUS DATA (AVERAGE NUMBER OF VEHICLES PER DAY AT SELECTED LOCATIONS)

Road Segment	1948	1953	1958	1961
Mile 47–Port Loko	27	80	200–300	100–200
Mange Ferry	9	25	50–100	50–100
Port Loko–Batkanu	12	20	50–100	50–100
Batkanu–Gbendembu	16	24	0–50	0–50
Gbendembu–Makeni	16	24	50–100	50–100
Makeni–Magburaka	23	40	200–300	200–300
Magburaka–Yele	22	27	50–100	100–200
Yele–Bo	20	46	100–200	100–200
Kumrabai–Yele	14	34	50–100	100–200
Bumpe–Bo	17	34	0–50	50–100
Bo–Koribundu	58	168	100–200	100–200
Koribundu–Pujehun	27	43	50–100	50–100
Pujehun–Potoru	26	32	50–100	50–100
Potoru–Zimi	10	19	0–50	0–50
Kenema–Giema	15	48	100–200	100–200
Lago–Lalehun	10	47	100–200	300–400
Bunumbu–Pendembu	7	22	50–100	50–100
Freetown–Waterloo	—	—	300–400	400–500
Waterloo–Mile 47	—	—	300–400	400–500
Bunumbu–Sefadu	—	—	200–300	100–200

SOURCE: Annual Reports of the Public Works Department.

constructed by the local people for their own use and in a small way showed that
significant changes could result from local initiative. Serving as feeders to the
national network, the hundreds of miles of new short stretches opened up large
areas, many for the first time (Figure 5). However, the District Councils failed to
continue as effective local development agencies with the completion of the five-
year plans, although they remained as corporate bodies responsible for a limited
range of local services.

During the 1950's, visible progress was slow in terms of miles of new later-
ite roads (Figure 6). However, startling and costly changes were effected: the main
colony-protectorate link was paved for a distance of approximately 80 miles from

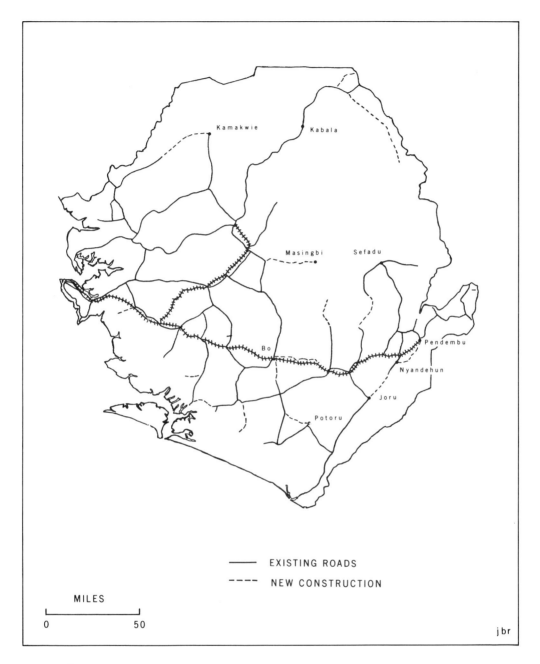

Figure 7.   Transport Network, 1967

Freetown into the heart of the protectorate, and the first major bridges appeared. Despite the fact that such works occupied much of the plant and staff of the Public Works Department and thus slowed or halted progress on other roads, the impact was dramatic. The higher traffic densities resulting from the increased speed of travel by roads often far outstripped the efficient carrying capacity of the roads and introduced the problem of sharply rising maintenance costs (Table 4).[54]

Since independence there have been marked and most important additions to the road system, but the basic structure of the network remains unaltered. A new paved road has been completed, linking Masingbi to Jaiama Sewafe, and within a few years it will probably become the most trafficked route in the country, as it provides a direct link between the diamond fields of Kono and the capital at Freetown. Other additions include the paving of the Mile 47–Lunsar and the Tagrin Point–Lungi roads, the construction of new roads from Bo to Baoma and from Kangahun to Panguma, and the new paved link between the villages of Nyandehun and Pendembu (Figure 7). The railway will probably be phased out of existence in the near future,[55] but all proposals to eliminate the line also stress the importance of improving the road links in the same direction and thus preserving the essential orientation and structure of the network.[56]

Conclusion

In the period since the British declaration of a protectorate in 1896, a modern transportation network has evolved, first by the extension of the rail line through the heart of the country and the expansion of its hinterland by the construction of feeder roads. Later the feeders were tied together, new links were built, and a national network of roads evolved to structure the geographic space of Sierra Leone. Because of the orientation of these road links, the country has been focused

54. Sierra Leone, Director of Public Works, *1956 Report of the Public Works Department,* p. 8.

55. Col. A. T. Juxon-Smith, *Statement on the Budget for 1967/68* (Freetown: Government Printer, 1967), pp. 9–10; *West Africa,* July 20, 1968, reports that the new civilian government will continue the same policy.

56. Transportation Consultants Inc., *Transport Survey of Sierra Leone* (Washington, D.C.: Transportation Consultants Inc., 1963); Italconsult, *Land Transport Survey: 10-Year Investment Programme (Interim Report)* (Rome: Italconsult, 1967); and Sierra Leone, Department of Works, Highway Division, "Paper on the Italconsult Study," mimeo. (Freetown, December, 1967).

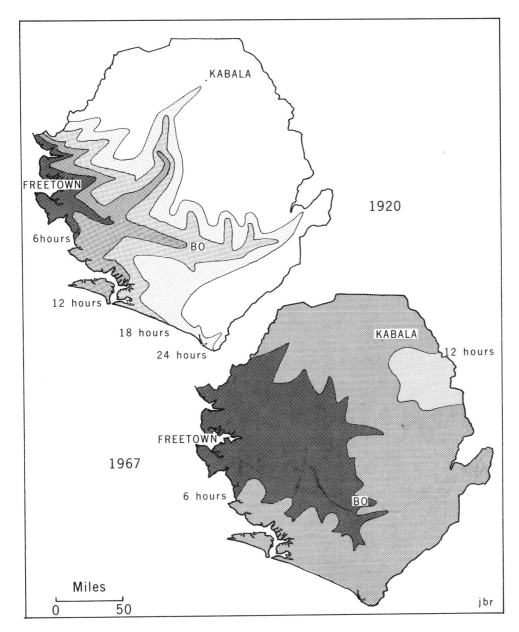

Figure 8.   Time-Distance to Freetown, 1920 and Present

upon Freetown and its port and upon the east-west axis defined by the rail route. Isolated local tribal systems have been tied together and the area within the country's political bounds has been welded together by the evolution of a national transport system (Figure 8).

Transport network growth has been a recursive process and the decisions and investments made during any given period were largely the outgrowth of the system as it existed in the previous time period. The fixed rail line and the system of feeder roads were the basis of the evolution of the system, and their influence is still felt in the zigzag pattern of roads along the main east-west transport axis of the country. The network grew as a reflection of colonial policy, and even today it retains a more or less treelike structure, acting like a river system to drain the products of the country from the interior to the principal port at Freetown. Geographic space has been provided with a highly specific fabric defined by the axes of movement and the urban-administrative hierarchy. It is within this fabric that ideas spread, that people move, that services are located, and within which modernity begins to emerge.

Diffusion: Institutions
of Modernization

The revolutionary change in man's way of life in modern times, which for several centuries was confined principally to the Western peoples, has in our lifetime come to affect all of mankind. For the first time in history, a universal pattern of modernity is emerging from the wide diversity of traditional values and institutions.[1]

The railway drove a wedge of cash-register values through the country. . . . Up the roads came hints of a wider more expansive life.[2]

In many ways, Sierra Leone remains the same today as it was a century ago. Tribal society continues as the dominant form of social organization. Communities remain isolated and largely unaware of the wider world. Agricultural techniques have changed but slightly. Disease, hunger, and malnutrition continue as daily problems. The subsistence economy predominates.

Yet within this pattern of apparent stagnation, hints of change occur, and in some areas, especially in the new towns and cities, revolutionary alterations have been and are being made. Often the changes are subtle; yet frequently they are dramatic, involving changes in the institutions and behavioral patterns of the society. Unlike former days, when people moved to clear new fields, to conquer their neighbors, or to flee the invader, they act today in response to the new foci of change, the towns and the cities. Modern transport systems extend the length and breadth of the country, bringing new ideas, new methods, and new people even to the most remote corners. A rudimentary national health service exists, and dispensaries, health centers, and occasionally a hospital and doctor can be found in the provincial towns. The school is now a familiar institution in the countryside, and education is usually highly esteemed. New organizations exist for the marketing of crops and the purchasing of daily needs. Postal services, though often slow and inefficient, are nearly ubiquitous. Information is disseminated by newspaper and radio, while in Freetown television is in limited use. National and local development plans have been formulated and implemented.

1. C. E. Black, "Change as a Condition of Modern Life," in *Modernization: The Dynamics of Growth,* ed. M. Weiner (New York: Basic Books, 1966), p. 17.
2. R. Lewis, *Sierra Leone: A Modern Portrait* (London: H.M.S.O., 1954), p. 151.

These changes, which affect all spheres of life—political, social, economic, and psychological—constitute the modernization process. Rather than being susceptible to exact definition, modernization may be characterized as a process whereby traditional institutions, methods, and patterns of life are adapted to or replaced by new, more modern forms.

> Historically, modernization is the process of change toward those types of social, economic and political systems that have developed in Western Europe and North America from the seventeenth century to the nineteenth century and have then spread.[3]

Each of the several dimensions of the complex process is the focus of separate, but often overlapping, disciplinary concerns.[4] Economists consider the application of technology to resources in order to instigate a growth of output per capita. Sociologists and social anthropologists are concerned with the complex set of social changes. Political scientists emphasize the problem of nation- and government-building.[5] Others, such as David McClelland, studying modernization from a psychological viewpoint, focus upon the attainment of an achievement motivation.[6] Cyril Black, a historian, stresses the increase of information and the ability to profitably employ that knowledge.[7] The geographer, relying upon spatial perspectives rather than distinctive subject matter, offers new insights into the diffusion of modernization by indicating the areal patterns of order and organization underlying the process and by indicating the spatial similarities and interactions of its several subprocesses.[8]

3. S. N. Eisenstadt, *Modernization: Protest and Change* (Englewood Cliffs, N.J.: Prentice-Hall, 1966), p. 1.

4. R. A. Lystad, ed., *The African World: A Survey of Social Research* (New York: Praeger, 1965).

5. M. Weiner, "Introduction," in *Modernization: The Dynamics of Growth,* pp. 3–4.

6. D. C. McClelland, "The Impetus to Modernize," *ibid.,* pp. 28–39.

7. C. E. Black, *The Dynamics of Modernization: A Study in Comparative History* (New York: Harper & Row, 1966).

8. E. Soja, *The Geography of Modernization in Kenya* (Syracuse: Syracuse University Press, 1968).

Modernization is a spatial-diffusion process, assuming patterns of varying intensity and rate. Its origins are localized to specific regions or zones, indexing a contact situation, and the patterns of change move like waves across the map, and cascade down the urban hierarchy as they are funneled along the transport system.[9]

Sierra Leone is not a uniform surface. Population is spread most unevenly, reflecting both patterns of rural settlement and the growing urban foci (see Figure 30). Change does not occur upon an isotropic surface but is channeled down the rivers and the paths and along the roads man has slowly carved on the map. The country has a fabric, defined not only by its environmental characteristics and the social system of its inhabitants, but also by the economic and administrative systems of the country. These several components of the fabric affect the pattern of the spatial diffusion of modernization. At times they operate individually, but usually in combination, to influence and direct the pattern of the spread of new techniques, new ideas, and new institutions.

Sierra Leone has evolved from a traditional, self-sufficient, colonial society, composed of numerous isolated units, to one of an evolving independent political, social, and economic system that is more akin to nations with higher standards of living and different social, political, and economic frameworks. Something new has been evolving—a unique combination of Western and African ideas, institutions, and ways of life.

The modernization process has been the direct result of the colonial experience. Britain, as the imperial power, was the agent of change, though in the early years a reluctant and often unintentional one. In a sense, her position posed a contradiction—not wanting to become involved in the intricacies of tribal society, but requiring modern administration and economics to incorporate the country into the imperial trading system, she built roads and a railway, extended communications, and established a health service.

9. T. Hagerstrand, "The Propagation of Innovation Waves," in *Lund Studies in Geography,* Ser. B, IV (1952), and R. L. Morrill, "Waves of Spatial Diffusion," *Journal of Regional Science,* VIII (1968), 1–18.

For many years British interests were confined largely to the Freetown settlement. Officially, there were few contacts with the interior until the latter half of the ninteenth century, and these were limited to punitive expeditions against warring chiefs, both to secure peaceful conditions for trade and to protect the colony from attack. However, by the latter years of the century, the competition for African trade was a vital issue in Europe. The Berlin Conference of 1885 defined spheres of influence as areas effectively occupied, and the French had secured control to the north and east. The British, in order to satisfy national prestige and to protect the interests of their trading firms operating out of Freetown and Bonthe, formally declared a protectorate over present-day Sierra Leone in 1896.[10] Administrative and medical officers were posted in the hinterland and construction of the railway began from Freetown. British influence upcountry became formal and effective.

Expense was the great problem of the early colonial government. Local sources had to supply the costs of administration by customs dues, taxes, and license fees, and, as a result, monies were unavailable for grand schemes of development. The "mother country" would not pay for the dramatic changes required to effect broad social and economic benefits for the local populace.

> The conception was that of a trusteeship. The Colonies like children under a trust, were to have every kind of help and encouragement; but out of their own funds.[11]

As a result, surplus revenues, when available, were used for trade, communications, order, and peace. Other services—education, medicine, and so forth—were not entirely neglected, and schools were built, hospitals established, and new crops introduced. However, these efforts were secondary and residual.

In 1929 the Colonial Development Fund was established for financing various schemes of economic development in the colonies by loan or grant. Unfortunately the monies were limited, and the basic intention was to "promote com-

10. Small territorial adjustments were also made with French Guinea in 1904 and with Liberia in 1911.

11. Joyce Cary, *Britain and West Africa* (London: Longmans, Green, 1946), p. 51.

merce with, or industry in, the United Kingdom" by assisting the development of agriculture and industries in the colonies.[12] Things such as education were outside the scope of the act.

By 1940 colonial policy was radically revised. Britain expanded her role beyond that of trustee and became actively engaged in promoting the development of resources and the welfare of the peoples of the colonies with the enactment of the Colonial Development and Welfare Act. In 1946, with the termination of the war, the program was greatly expanded, and, by independence in 1961, a total of £8,198,677 had been invested in health, education, communications, and transportation facilities.[13]

Thus any discussion of the colonial effects upon modernization and development must be time-specific. Prior to 1929, the colony operated exclusively on its own resources and only limited funds were provided for certain kinds of development during the 1930's. Policy was changed in 1940, but it was not until after 1946 that funds became available for the relatively massive developmental inputs which characterized the 1950's.

The analysis of the spread of modernization requires surrogate measures indexing the complex economic, social, political, and psychological processes. Though the actual location of a school does not measure change, the incidence of schools and the altering of behavioral patterns are so correlated as to be virtually synonymous.[14] Similarly, the location of a post office does not measure the actual level of communications, but the fact of location indicates a localized demand or reflects the colonial economic and administrative systems as they evolved.

While the growth of the transport system is part of the modernization

12. "Selections from 'Statement of Policy on Colonial Development and Welfare,' Presented by the Secretary of State for the Colonies to Parliament, February 1940," Appendix D of *Survey of British Commonwealth Affairs*, Vol. II: *Problems of Economic Policy 1918–1939, Part II*, by W. K. Hancock (London: Oxford University Press, 1942), p. 344.

13. Great Britain, *Colonial Development and Welfare Acts: Return of Schemes* (annual series of papers).

14. D. L. Sumner, *Education in Sierra Leone* (Freetown: Government Printer, 1963).

process, it is also much more. The spreading network of rail and roads continually redefines the spatial fabric of the country in which health services are located, schools are opened, communications are structured, ideas spread, and new ways of life emerge. The network acts with the urban-administrative hierarchy as the very framework within which decisions affecting the process of change are made.

An overriding theme is the influence of these two emerging spatial systems—the network and hierarchy—on the spread of developmental infrastructure and social services. It is along the rivers, rail, and roads that the schools spread and it is through the urban system that health services are provided. There is a positive feedback, with the towns and the roads being part of the diffusion process yet at the same time directing and influencing the pattern.

Spatial aspects of the modernization process in Sierra Leone are illustrated by the diffusion of a number of institutions and a complex set of indices which, though not comprising the whole of the modernization process, certainly reflect it.[15] Each index and institution has unique origins and characteristics, yet the strength of the fabric and the highly complex interactions among the indices lead to general areal patterns.

NATIVE ADMINISTRATION[16]

With the declaration of the protectorate over the hinterland in 1896, the British imposed an administrative structure which can be characterized as a system of

15. Although historical census materials are lacking, both in quality and areal coverage, certain non-parametric data are available. Information on the location and date of establishment of facilities such as schools, dispensaries, and roads can be derived from a wide variety of sources. Whenever programs were initiated, the background, expectations, and proposals were sent to the Colonial Office. Expansion in the number of hospitals, banks, roads, etc., were cited in the annual governor's address to the Legislative Council. Reports of district officers contained or summarized in the Annual Protectorate Reports cite important local developments in all spheres, and the annual reports of the various departments—Public Works, Health, etc.—indicate changes in the numbers and locations of facilities. Other sources such as histories, development plans, and incidental reports add further to the data base, as do items in the weekly *Gazette*.

16. Much of the background material for this section was derived from M. Kilson, *Politi-*

indirect rule. Five district officers, each with small supporting staffs, were assigned to superintend 27,000 square miles of roadless country. Naturally their primary concern was not the imposition of an immediate control over the native peoples of the protectorate, but rather the securing of conditions conducive to European trade and enterprise.[17] Order was to be assured and investment safeguarded. The traditional rulers continued as the heads of the local social and political systems and were incorporated as the lowest rung in the administrative hierarchy. The system remained intact for a period of 40 years, though in a small way the British attempted to improve the outlook and efficiency of the traditional authorities by the establishment of the Bo School in 1906 for the sons and nominees of chiefs. The school was to train the future leaders in the ways of modern farming, bridge-building, road-making, and administration:

> The basic philosophy in establishing and maintaining such exclusive educational institutions is that if the experiment of establishing successful Native Administration is to succeed, the natural rulers of the people cannot remain the most conservative elements in the community, blind to the new world in which they live.[18]

In the early years the political control exerted by the indigenous rulers was adequate, given the simplified local circumstances. By the 1930's, however, with the changes induced by the provision of law and order and the construction of a railway and roads, the system of protectorate administration was no longer suitable. The simple form of indirect rule was more appropriate to controlling backward populations than to facilitating change and development. Problems such as sanitation, water supply, and welfare were increasing, and with the growth of urban centers the influx of strangers was causing new problems. If there was to be meaningful development, much of it had to come from the chiefdom level, and tra-

cal Change in a West African State: A Study of the Modernization Process in Sierra Leone (Cambridge: Harvard University Press, 1966); and Lord Hailey, Native Administration in the British African Territories, Part III: West Africa (London: H.M.S.O., 1951).

17. M. Crowder, West Africa under Colonial Rule (London: Hutchinson; Evanston, Ill.: Northwestern University Press, 1968).

18. Sumner, Education in Sierra Leone, pp. 140–41.

ditional authorities were not organized to erect dispensaries and schools, repair bridges, and construct roads. The budgetary advantages of the old system to the colonial power were often largely offset by the large private claims chiefs were permitted to make upon local sources of revenue, thus reducing the capacity of the chiefdom to undertake any form of development project.

> In particular, the role given to traditional authorities was too limited; they were organized mainly to handle problems of law and order, with their main responsibility for direct assistance to modern socio-economic change being limited to labor recruitment for public works and tax collection.[19]

In 1935 the government sent J. S. Fenton, a district commissioner, to Nigeria to observe the operation of the Native Administration system in effect there and to report on its possible effectiveness and implementation in Sierra Leone.[20] Fenton's report strongly encouraged the adoption of the system and emphasized its ability to provide funds for local development and to allow for a wider participation in the political process. Legislation, following the procedure of the Native Authority Laws of Nigeria and Tanganyika, was embodied in three ordinances enacted in 1937.[21] Chiefdom treasuries were established, taxing authority was provided, and the power to enact bylaws and issue orders in pursuance of social services and development projects was given.

The new system was not imposed everywhere, but rather was encouraged and promoted by the district officers. The final decision to "modernize" lay with the people, especially the chiefs, the only other stipulation being that a chiefdom be large enough and prosperous enough to support an administrative and developmental budget.

Fenton, in his report, suggested that the plan start in certain model

19. Kilson, *Political Change,* p. 18.
20. Sierra Leone, *Sessional Paper* No. 3, 1935, *Report by Mr. J. S. Fenton, O.B.E., District Commissioner, on a Visit to Nigeria and on the Application of the Principles of Native Administration to the Protectorate of Sierra Leone.*
21. The Tribal Authorities Ordinance (No. 8 of 1937), the Chiefdom Tax Ordinance (No. 10 of 1937), and the Chiefdom Treasuries Ordinance (No. 11 of 1937).

chiefdoms which would serve as examples to other tribal authorities:

> If the suggestions are accepted, four Upper Mendi Chiefdoms, Bambarra, Mando, Jawi and Jaluahun might be persuaded to put them into practice. These chiefdoms are governed by educated chiefs, their people are prosperous and progressive, they are of sufficient size each to have their own treasury, and they are accessible by road and railway and so may afterwards serve as models.[22]

Two model Native Administrations were established in 1936 and given statutory basis in 1937.

TABLE 5. PROGRESS OF ESTABLISHMENT OF NATIVE ADMINISTRATIONS

Year	Total	Year	Total
1936	2	1950	139
1938	34	1952	147
1940	70	1954	146[a]
1942	97	1956	143[a]
1944	107	1958	144
1946	118	1960	145
1948	128	1967	146

SOURCE: *Protectorate Handbook*, 1962.
[a]Reduction in total due to the amalgamation of existing N.A.'s.

The idea spread rapidly, but did not take hold everywhere immediately (Table 5). Many chiefdoms were too small and too poor to be effective and were gradually eliminated through amalgamation upon the decision of the people, usually at the death of a chief. Many chiefs were originally opposed to the arrangement, for under the old system their local powers were supreme and their income, based upon customary dues and obligations, was large. To overcome resistance the colonial government compromised by making the share of Native Administration revenue available to the chiefs excessively large.

22. Sierra Leone, *Report by Mr. J. S. Fenton*, p. 43.

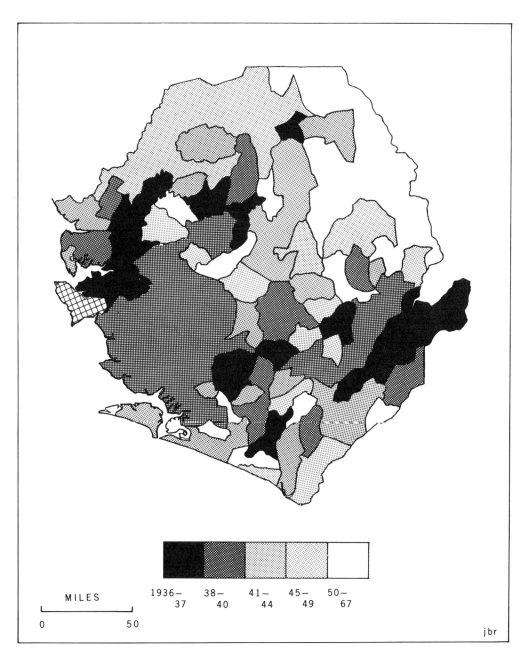

Figure 9.   Dates of Establishment of Native Administrations, by Chiefdom

        From the model chiefdoms in the far east of the country the idea quickly
spread by demonstration effects, by personal information and contact, and by the
urgings of the district officers (Figure 9). The larger, more prosperous chiefdoms
and those most exposed to "modern" influences adopted most readily. These
included those chiefdoms extending along the transport system, having at least a

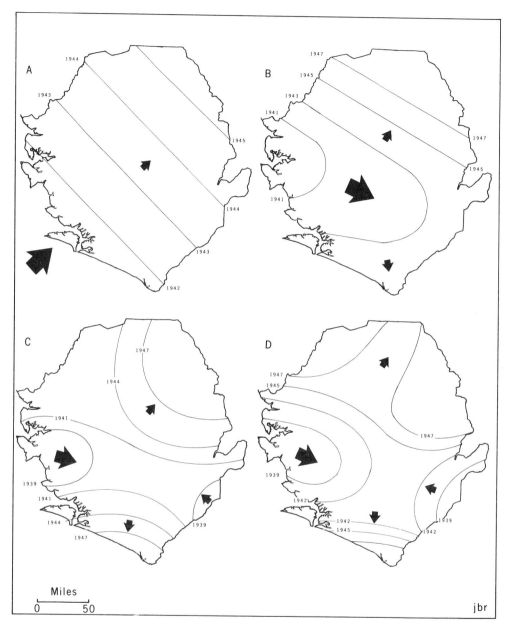

Figure 10.   Diffusion of Native Administrations:
A—Linear Trend Surface; B—Quadratic Trend Surface; C—Cubic Trend Surface; D—Quartic Trend Surface

few schools, and being involved in the money economy. The laggards were the small and isolated chiefdoms; the larger late adopters, such as Nieni, Mongo, and Neya in Koinadugu District, represent amalgams of as many as five smaller units.

The general spatial pattern can be clarified and refined by a process of filtering local anomalies from the map pattern. By trend surface mapping,[23] the small-scale local components are removed and the resultant surface represents the higher-scale regional component of the map. The technique is similar to fitting a curve to a set of points on a two-dimensional graph by the use of least-squares regression methods, but differs in that it is applied to a three-dimensional map surface. The effect is to sacrifice local information, or to reduce local irregularities, to produce a clearer picture of the over-all trend.

The most dominant linear trend is a progression of acceptance inland from the coast in a southwest to northeast direction (Figure 10). The first-order surface represents a mapping of the regression plane:

$$Y - \beta_0 + \beta_1 X_1 + \beta_2 X_2$$

and the general expression for the higher-order surfaces may be represented by:

$$Y = \beta_0 + \beta_1 X_1 + \beta_2 X_2 + \beta_3 X_1^2 + \beta_4 X_1 X_2 + \beta_5 X_2^2 \\ + \beta_6 X_1^3 + \beta_7 X_1^2 X_2 + \beta_8 X_1 X_2^2 + \beta_9 X_2^3 + \dots$$

where Y represents the date of establishment of Native Administration, and X_1 represents the latitude, X_2 the longitude, of the main town of the chiefdom.

Since the first-order surface accounts for only a small fraction of the variance, a series of higher-order polynomial surfaces were fitted in the same manner (Figure 10). Successive warpings of the surface provide greater detail to the over-all trend by incorporating the influence of the main line of the railway, the demonstration chiefdoms, and the northern branch line. The fraction of explained variance increases from 4 per cent for the linear surface to 16, 30, and 38 per cent, and greater detail is given to the general spatial trend. Beyond the fourth-order surface, subsequent higher-order polynomials provide closer fits to the actual data pattern but reduce the generality of the surface and diminish the strength of the regional trend. Most apparent is the influence of the railway, with diffusion effects

23. R. J. Chorley and P. Haggett, "Trend Surface Mapping in Geographical Research," *Transactions of the Institute of British Geographers*, **XXXVII** (1965), 47–67.

spreading from the early model chiefdoms in the east and from Freetown in the west, before reaching northward along the branch line.

While the effects were limited, the Native Administrations provided an opportunity to participate in the administering of local government and small-scale development schemes, if only as a clerk, bookkeeper, or laborer. Their local development role was pre-empted in 1950 by the larger District Councils, and much of their development revenue was diverted to the Councils to implement their local development plans. However, the spread of Native Administrations indexes the general course of modernization at the chiefdom scale and provides a measure of local attitudes and readiness to accept change and modernization.

MEDICAL FACILITIES

Perhaps the most constraining factor on African development, yet one often ignored, is the prevalence of disease, sickness, and malnutrition. Despite very real advances, malaria remains endemic, outbreaks of yaws, sleeping sickness, and smallpox are frequent, and malnutrition ranging from starvation to specific dietary deficiencies affects virtually the entire population. Much has been done of a prophylactic nature as hospitals, dispensaries, and treatment centers have been established, eradication programs implemented, and sanitation improved. Yet in many parts of the country the pace of life remains geared to the flux of disease; men suffer frequently from hunger, and infant-mortality rates remain shockingly high.

Existing facilities and personnel are totally insufficient. There is only one doctor for every 14,800 people, one trained midwife for every 22,600, and one dentist for every 218,400.[24] Yet even these meager rates are signs of advance; only a few years ago there were no doctors, nurses, or dentists.

The description and analysis of the extension of medical and health facilities in Sierra Leone is difficult because of the lack of any substantive background materials and documentary sources other than administrative reports. Specific

24. J. I. Clarke, *Sierra Leone in Maps* (London: University of London Press, 1966), p. 66.

information on the changing areal patterns of disease, mortality, and malnutrition are simply not available. However, data recording responsive spatial decisions do exist for the growth of medical facilities, the opening of hospitals, the postings of medical personnel, and the operations of treatment centers. Such data, when mapped, suggest certain generalizations about the spatial pattern of the provision of medical facilities.

The spatial principles organizing and arranging the areal patterning and extension of health services varied over time as administrative priorities changed and financial constraints loosened. In the protectorate the early medical facilities exactly reflected the colonial administrative hierarchy, as medical personnel were located primarily to serve the district officers and their staffs. As such, they reflect the principle of space-packing or area-filling, with services located evenly in space to provide a broad areal coverage over the protectorate, whose population distribution and other geographic properties were virtually unknown at the time. Locations shifted as the administrative system responded to more realistic perceptions of population distribution and to the space-shrinking effect of the construction of the railway. Gradually the several mission societies began to provide medical services in areas not well served by the government institutions. Then, as the objectives of the medical service were redefined and the provision of health care to the local people was given a higher priority, a functional hierarchy of medical services emerged, partially independent of the administrative system. The hospitals were located in the district headquarters, but dispensaries and health centers were opened in the larger towns, near the hospitals. Mobile facilities served the constantly changing requirements occasioned by the sporadic outbreak of disease.

In 1896, at the declaration of the protectorate over the hinterland of Sierra Leone, general hospitals and smaller, specialized facilities for smallpox and incurable diseases existed at the capital of Freetown and the major trading port of Bonthe (Figure 11). Several dispensaries were located in the colony villages and at a few of the smaller coastal customs stations to provide at least a modicum of services. In the protectorate, medical facilities were limited to the United Brethren in Christ (U.B.C.) mission station at Rotifunk and the medical officers stationed at

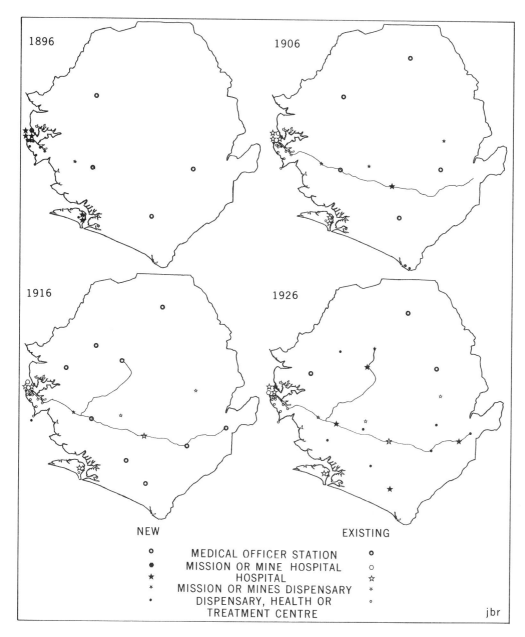

Figure 11.   Establishment of Medical Facilities, 1896 to 1926

four of the five district headquarters.[25] Some of the stations were closed briefly during the Hut Tax War of 1898, but by 1906 they were open again. A major hospital also opened at Bo and medical mission stations were established at Shenge, Taiama, and Jaiama.

The pattern continued to the 1930's, with the few locational alterations

25. A medical officer was assigned to the fifth headquarters at Falaba in 1900.

reflecting the reorganization of the administrative regions and centers of the protectorate. The Connaught Hospital opened in Freetown in 1922 to replace the Colonial Hospital destroyed by fire two years earlier, and in 1924 the European Hospital began work, though, as its name implies, not for the general public. The only marked improvements during the period were the establishment of medical missions by the American Wesleyans at Kamabai, the terminus of the branch line, and by the Methodists at Segbwema, near the farthest extension of the main line. During the 1930's these stations, as well as those of the U.B.C. mission at Jaiama and Taiama, expanded to full hospitals.

Though not immediately evident from visual inspection of the maps, the attitude of the colonial administration determined the pattern and intensity of the provision of health care facilities to the local peoples. Primarily their attention focused upon the provision of medical services for the government personnel and stations. As funds were limited and such provisions were expensive, the people were largely ignored.

> It is something that we are able to keep open ten medical stations in the Protectorate, but what is that in an area of 27,000 square miles with a population of one and a half millions? The problem of extending medical aid to the millions of natives of West Africa is indeed so vast that considerations of finance altogether preclude it, for many years to come, being tackled by the necessarily very large staff of fully qualified male and female doctors that would be required.[26]

Yet during the 1930's the colonial attitude gradually changed. By 1939, with the lifting of the depression, the administration considered the extension of medical facilities in the protectorate and drafted a five-year plan.

> The inadequacy of medical facilities in the Protectorate . . . has been given serious consideration and a five-year plan of extension has been drawn up. The plan provides for the establishment of sixteen new dispensaries, for the better equipping and staffing of existing hospitals and a very considerable enlargement of the hospitals at Bo and Makeni.[27]

26. Sierra Leone, *Legislative Council Debates, 1925,* "Address of the Governor."
27. Sierra Leone, *Legislative Council Debates, 1939–40,* "Appendix to the Address by the Governor."

The outbreak of the war caused a serious curtailment of the plan and the sleeping sickness epidemic in the Kailahun District used up the limited available funds. Few new facilities opened—several treatment centers in the Eastern Province as part of the sleeping sickness campaign, two new dispensaries, and new buildings for two previously existing dispensaries and for the Bonthe and Pujehun hospitals.

At the end of the war, health services grew quickly under the financing of the revised Colonial Development and Welfare scheme. Four new hospitals and 50 health centers were to be constructed over the next ten years to provide health facilities for the entire population. "When this programme is completed no individual should be more than 10 miles from some form of medical assistance."[28] Each protectorate district would have a hospital in the main town and health centers would be located in all the other important urban centers.

However, the immediate postwar years were a time of disappointment. Three of the existing protectorate hospitals had to be closed intermittently because of staff shortages, and the progress of the health center scheme was slow because of lack of materials and technical and supervisory staff. By 1952, none of the planned hospitals and only six of the health centers had been opened. The only signs of advancement were the expansion of the endemic diseases control program and the increasing role played by the newly formed District Councils in the operation of the protectorate dispensaries.[29] The 1950's, however, were years of much more rapid progress. The shortages of the immediate postwar years were overcome, and by 1957 the four new hospitals were open and health centers provided at the majority of larger towns. At the same time, the medical missions expanded their operations, opening numerous dispensaries in several parts of the country as well as a few new hospitals (Figure 12).

Recognizing the primal importance of health and medical services, the newly independent government prepared a National Health Plan, and imple-

28. Sierra Leone, *Annual Report of the Medical Department, 1947*, p. 4.
29. Expenditure on health and medical services remained ridiculously low. Annual per capita finances available approximated three shillings, as compared to eight pounds in the U.K.

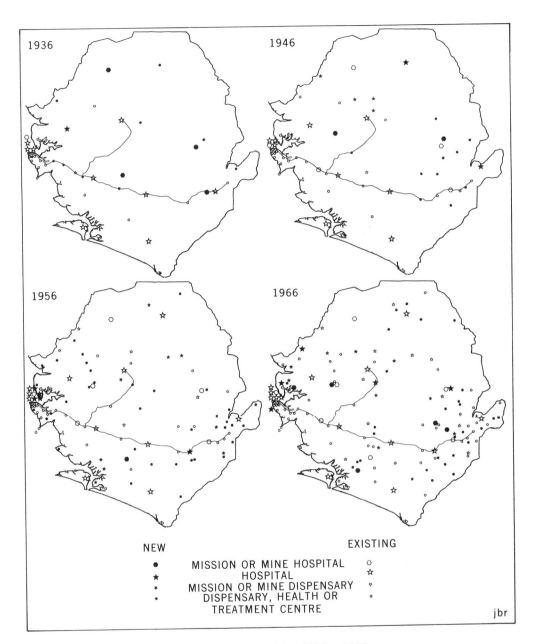

Figure 12.   Establishment of Medical Facilities, 1936 to 1966

mentation began in 1962.[30] The plan called for marked expansion in medical services and proposed a strengthening of the existing hierarchical areal pattern of
provision of health services. The base hospitals at Bo and Freetown were to be
improved to serve as the foundation of a system of rural hospitals in each of the

30. Sierra Leone, *Development Plan of the Health Care Services of Sierra Leone*
(Freetown, May, 1962).

district headquarters. Provision was also made for an ancillary network of health centers in each of the chiefdoms. The system was augmented by the mobile Endemic Diseases Control Units for the mass treatment of sleeping sickness, yaws, and leprosy and by the many dispensaries operated by the District Councils.

The post-independence results, especially in terms of new facilities and new areas served, are indeed impressive. Over the past few years the hospital services have improved and the number of health centers has more than doubled. Yet the story is not yet complete. Many areas are devoid of services; several of the dispensaries and health centers lack sufficient or adequate staff. The data on doctors, however, are most indicative; although there are far more doctors in Sierra Leone today than there were in the years prior to independence, and far more of these are Sierra Leoneans, there are actually fewer in the provinces.

PRIMARY EDUCATION[31]

Primary education is an index of modernization somewhat different from the set of indices so far considered, being largely outside the confines of governmental policy in terms of its locational references.

> There is a good deal of truth in the statement by some authorities that the work of education was begun and for many years carried forward almost exclusively by missionary effort and that had there been no missionaries there would have been at any rate, until modern times, little African education.[32]

Rather than representing the unified action of one corporate body, the growth of educational facilities depicts the effects of over 15 separate voluntary organizations operating over a time period spanning 175 years and interacting with one another and under varying degrees of government regulation and control.

31. The kind co-operation of the Education Department and its staff is gratefully acknowledged.

32. Sierra Leone, Education Department, *Triennial Survey, 1955–57*, p. 2.

Yet the over-all diffusion pattern is highly regular in its areal expression and quite strongly reflects the influence of the evolving transportation system.

Sierra Leone has been termed "the Athens of Africa," and in a historical sense the appellation is well deserved. The colony was the site of the earliest educational endeavors in Africa, as well as the location of the first African college—Fourah Bay—founded in 1827.[33] Educational efforts probably began with the first settlement of freed slaves, though the earliest official school was begun in 1792 by a schoolmaster sent out from England by the Sierra Leone Company.[34] Education was quickly established in the colony, as many of its residents originated in places where education had been regarded as a badge of distinction. By 1826 there were 22 schools in the colony with an attendance of slightly over 2,000 pupils.[35] Most were organized and supported by Christian missions, though the government provided some schooling for the newly landed freed slaves through the operations of the Liberated African Department. Much of the zeal for school expansion was a result of competition among the several mission societies rather than of the educational wants and needs of the people themselves. By 1841 the number of schools had almost doubled to 42, and from that time continued to increase, though fluctuating in number from year to year, as five new mission societies entered the field.[36]

> The denominational competition in opening schools paid no regard to either educational planning or continuity of effort; a school may be opened today and closed tomorrow, as long as the incident lent excitement to the game.[37]

Meanwhile, the penetration of education with the missions into the hinterland beyond the colony lagged far behind. There had been a short-lived mission

33. Although originally founded to train African clergy, teachers, and lay workers, the college officially affiliated with the University of Durham in 1876 and continued the connection until it recently became a separate university.

34. Sumner, *Education in Sierra Leone*, p. 5.

35. *Ibid.*, p. 50.

36. *Ibid.*, p. 52.

37. *Ibid.*, p. 75.

station and school on the Bullom shore, just north of Freetown, in the early years of the nineteenth century. Later, in 1840, a concerted effort was made to establish the Temne mission, based at Port Loko, but it closed after ten years as a result of opposition and indifference by the predominantly Muslim people. The level of success in the colony was high; a station in the hinterland usually meant death or debilitation for the missionaries.

The first large-scale and successful penetration of the hinterland occurred in the non-Muslim country along the coast to the south of the colony. An American mission, the United Brethren in Christ, opened its headquarters at Shenge in 1855, and within a few years the surrounding area was dotted with churches and schools. In 1877 a base was opened further inland up the Bumpe River at Rotifunk, and in a short time it became the center for the hinterland mission. Gradually other missions followed the example of the U.B.C. and opened mission stations and schools upcountry, though not with the same areal intensity. By 1898 there were 31 schools in the protectorate, two-thirds of which were U.B.C.[38] However, the 1898 Hut Tax War effectively wiped out most of the educational effort in the protectorate. Missionaries, teachers, and their adherents were either forced to flee or were killed, and the center of the educational, as well as the medical, effort in the interior at Rotifunk was destroyed and burned to the ground.

However, the effects of the rising lasted only a short time, and most of the schools were reopened—though the missions abandoned many of their more distant stations. In 1907 there were 23 schools open in the protectorate, of which 19 belonged to the U.B.C.[39] With the building of the railway inland from Freetown, the missions took advantage of the new communications link and opened schools all along the line. As the feeder roads extended from the rail line, they too became the loci of schools. Thus the period before the Second World War was a time of transport-oriented educational expansion. The first schools opened along the coast, which provided a base line for later penetration up the rivers. With the extension

38. *Ibid.,* p. 118.
39. *Ibid.,* p. 134.

of the transport system, schools opened all along the rail line and expanded up the feeder roads. Since the railway and most roads were located in the south of the country, the effect was a further sharpening of the north-south educational differential, originally caused by the Muslim resistance to mission efforts in the north. In effect, the Muslim religion acted as a semipermeable barrier to the spread of schools, with the result that in 1937 there were 143 schools in the southern half of the country and only 26 in the north.[40]

Until this time protectorate education was almost exclusively the concern of the missions, with the government operating only a few special schools and providing small grants to roughly half the mission schools. The 1937 sessional paper on educational policy in the protectorate recommended the establishment of some government schools and noted the striking north-south differential, but even the proposed schools "should be regarded as a temporary measure; they should as a rule be opened only in those areas unserved by missionary activity and with the deliberate intention of handing them over to Native Administrations as these develop."[41]

After the war the overriding directional influence of the transportation system on the evolution of the pattern of schools weakened. Though the influence of road and rail remained pronounced, the period of transport control was over. Gradually the interstices between the main roads began to fill, and the Native Administrations, as well as some missions, began to open schools in areas away from the main roads. Competition among the several mission bodies began anew as their spreading areas of influence began to coalesce. The result was an apparent random opening and closing of schools, as new schools drew students away from previously existing institutions, often forcing them to close. Yet despite these new, nonspatial factors, the areal pattern of education was remarkably persistent. The diffusion process was contagious, with new schools tending to open in

40. Sierra Leone, *Sessional Paper* No. 5, 1937, *Educational Policy in the Protectorate,* p. 9.

41. *Ibid.,* p. 4.

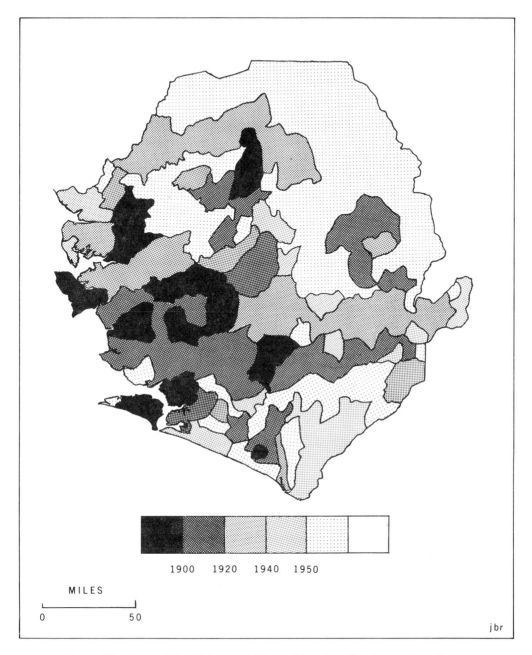

Figure 13.   Dates of Establishment of Primary Education: All Voluntary Agencies

close proximity to previously existing schools[42] and the Muslim north continuing to act as a semipermeable barrier to the areal spread.

42. The neighborhood effect often resulted in removing the pupil base from previously
existing schools. Legislation was put into effect to regulate the proximity of schools, but to little
avail.

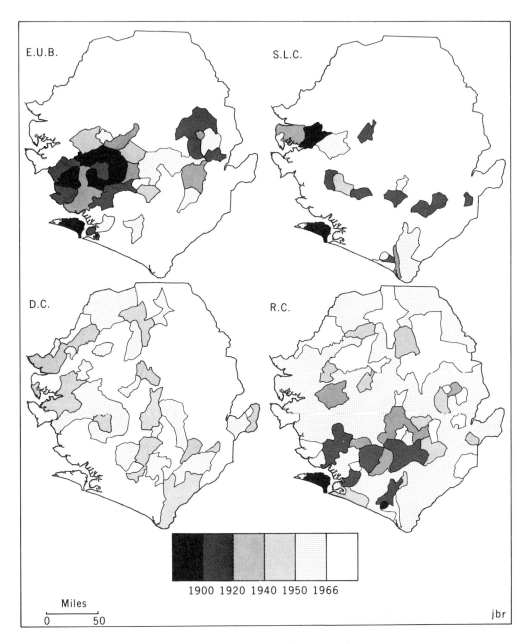

Figure 14.   Dates of Establishment of Primary Education: Selected Voluntary Agencies

To generalize the spatial pattern of diffusion of education, the data on the opening of more than a thousand schools have been smoothed by considering the date of establishment of the first school in each chiefdom (Figure 13). The generalized areal pattern highlights the broad spatial regularities identified previously: the north-south differential, the influence of the rail line, and the impact of the early coastal and riverine missions. There are many irregularities in the pattern, but

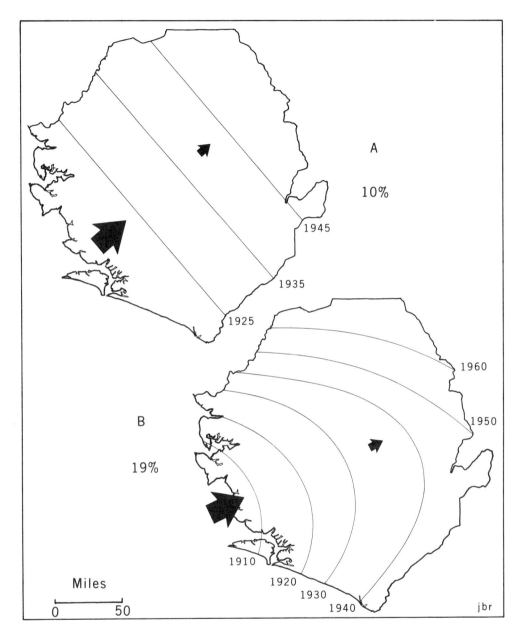

Figure 15.   Diffusion of Primary Education:
A—Linear Trend Surface; B—Quadratic Trend Surface

they are outweighed by the spatial trends. The order is evident despite the fact that the map represents a composite of the activities of fifteen mission societies as well as those of the local and national governments.

The over-all pattern, however, can be decomposed into its component parts by considering the same information for each of the voluntary agencies. Some, such as the Evangelical United Brethren (E.U.B.), show a precise areal coverage in a specific region. Other agencies, such as the Sierra Leone Church (S.L.C.), tend to operate mainly along the rail line and in the larger protectorate towns. Still others, such as the District Councils (D.C.) and Roman Catholics (R.C.), are spread widely across the map, reflecting for the D.C. schools the independent operation of many small agencies and for the R.C. schools an expansion from a core area (Figure 14).

In order to abstract and generalize the spatial pattern and pace of the process of educational expansion and to provide a basis of comparison with several of the other indices of modernization, trend surface analysis was used on the date-of-first-opening-by-chiefdom data as a further space-smoothing and generalizing device. The first-order surface depicts the strongest linear regional trend, a general progression inland from the coast. Successive higher-order surfaces provide further precision and show the north-south differential, the influence of the early coastal and riverine missions, and the effect of the railway (Figure 15). Obviously, much detail is filtered out—the second-order surface accounts for only 19 per cent of the variance in the original data—but the spatial regularities are clarified as the general "diffusion signal" is removed from the "background noise." Most important, however, the original statements on the strength of the fabric in directing the diffusion of modernization are substantiated; the effects of the transport system are dominant even in education, where many voluntary agencies have spread their influence from several distinct core areas.

SECONDARY EDUCATION[43]

The pattern of evolution of secondary-education facilities in Sierra Leone is quite dissimilar to that of the provision of primary schooling. Aside from the obvious time lag, the underlying principles defining the locational pattern have been very distinct. If schools are considered as central place functions with specific thresh-

43. For a review of secondary education in Sierra Leone, see E. D. Baker, "The Development of Secondary Education in Sierra Leone" (Ph.D. diss., University of Michigan, 1963).

olds and ranges,[44] then the respective values for secondary education are much greater than for primary. Because of the general low level of education, the secondary schools draw from wider areas; their locations, rather than being spread widely, are highly localized, especially in the larger urban places.

Secondary education in Sierra Leone dates to the founding of the Church Missionary Society Grammar School and the Female Institute in Freetown in 1845. Both ventures were highly successful and their list of graduates includes students attracted from all along the West African coast. By the turn of the century five secondary schools had been founded, all in Freetown and, with one exception, all operated by mission societies. Teaching tended to follow the classical English model, and it was not until 1904, with the opening of the Albert Academy, that more practical commercial and industrial training was offered.

Although the number of schools continued to increase, their areal pattern remained extremely concentrated, for until 1937 there were no secondary schools operating in the protectorate.[45] In that year the government expanded the Bo school to the secondary level, and at the end of the war the Harford School for Girls at Moyamba began to offer secondary training. Very gradually at first, but expanding rapidly in the late 1950's and early 1960's, secondary schools began to open in many of the larger protectorate towns (Figure 16). The diffusion may be characterized as a hierarchical process, with schools spreading through the urban system, as opposed to the spatially contagious nature of the spread of primary education. The evolution and present-day pattern of secondary education reflect the higher-order function of such schools.[46] With only minor exceptions, the pattern of secondary schools is the pattern of large towns, and only the north-south differential resulting from the religious differences causes marked deviation. The

44. W. Christaller, *Central Places in Southern Germany*, trans. C. W. Baskin (Englewood Cliffs, N.J.: Prentice-Hall, 1966).

45. The first seventeen schools opened in Sierra Leone were all located in Freetown.

46. In fact, Harvey found them to be one of the determinants in the definition of the urban hierarchy (M. E. E. Harvey, "A Geographical Study of the Pattern, Processes and Consequences of Urban Growth in Sierra Leone in the Twentieth Century" [Ph.D. diss., University of Durham, 1966]).

concentration in Freetown indicates the traditional and lasting importance of education in Creole society, as well as indexing the overwhelming primacy of the capital.

THE CO-OPERATIVE MOVEMENT[47]

Unlike many of the other indices of modernization, whose pace and progress have been directed by the government administration, the co-operative movement is an example of a more or less spontaneous development "from below." It is true that the origins lay with the activities of the government, but once the seeds of the idea were planted, it spread rapidly. Throughout the history of the co-operative movement in Sierra Leone, the popular requests for government support of societies has always far exceeded the ability of the Co-operative Department to train, administer, and supervise.

As an institution, the co-operative society is not radically different from existing forms of African social organization. The strong communal feeling which characterizes African society complements the ideas of co-operation. The West African delegates to the African conference in London in October, 1948, expressed their desire for co-operatives in preference to the emergence of large farmsteads or state-operated farms. They stated that any serious modification of the existing land-tenure system would be viewed with suspicion and would be disastrous.

> Co-operation provided a means whereby the existing African social organization of small holders would be retained and combined with the gradual education of the farmers in better methods, and it would permit the introduction of fertilisers, insecticides and machinery on a group basis.[48]

47. The author expresses a special note of thanks to Mr. Kombe-Bundu, Registrar, and Mr. Fofona, Deputy Registrar, of the Co-operative Department for so willingly providing access to materials. Without the kind and most helpful assistance of Mr. J. C. O. Williams, Assistant Registrar, the analysis of the co-operative movement would not have been possible.

48. Sierra Leone, *Report on Co-operation in Sierra Leone*, p. 2, quoted from the *Weekly Bulletin*, October 10, 1948.

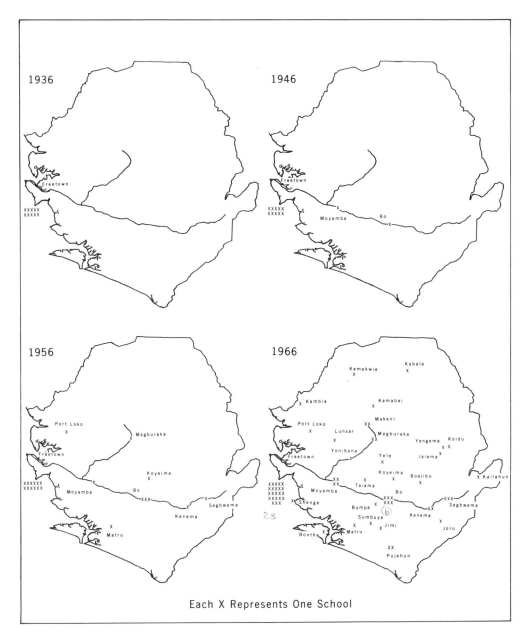

Figure 16.   Expansion of Secondary Education

The movement was a positive benefit to rural society. The quality of production improved as the marketing societies offered premium prices for better-
quality crops. An incentive was provided for increased production, not only
through generally higher prices but also by providing a means of owning machinery and transport and for buying tools and fertilizers. There have been several side
benefits as well. People have been trained in the elements of responsible democ-

racy at the local level, for they were provided with what may have been their first opportunity to express and implement their own ideas and to vote, regardless of their individual position in the traditional social structure. The movement also prepared, by means of marketing and buying institutions, a vehicle for the Africanization of trade and for training in basic business techniques. It has also become a vehicle of social welfare by encouraging community action toward common goals.

> The indirect good effects of cooperation are beginning to make themselves obvious. One is an increase of economic vigour. . . . People are working for themselves instead of for their creditors; and those who have done one job successfully with the help of their Society, are encouraged to tackle another. Some more of the energy released by getting out of debt is going into works of social welfare—meeting halls and stores, roads, better drinking water and the like.[49]

The movement originated in Sierra Leone as early as 1936, when a Farmers' Society was formed by the Department of Agriculture at Mambolo. The department's main objective was not the institution of co-operative societies but rather the increase of rice production for export and the improvement of the varieties of rice grown. The first society was an immediate success and the monetary benefits were a highly visible index. The idea quickly took hold, and an additional four such societies were formed within the next three years. However, the war years effectively cut off the markets and government support was redirected; the societies disappeared.

Nevertheless, such early seeds signaled a means of improving economic well-being while retaining traditional organization with but slightly altered methods. The demand for new societies quickly reappeared after the war, and efforts were made to open co-operative-type consumer shops in Kenema, Giema, and Rotifunk. A rice-producers' society was begun near Bunumbu, and the fishermen at Shenge actively promoted a fish-marketing society.[50] All these efforts were

49. Sierra Leone, Co-operative Department, "1954 Report for the Protectorate Handbook," department file P3/1/5.
50. Sierra Leone, *Report on Co-operation*, p. 4.

TABLE 6. GROWTH OF THE CO-OPERATIVE MOVEMENT (ANNUAL NUMBER OF SOCIETIES BY DISTRICT)

Year	Bo	Moyamba	Bonthe	Pujehun	Kailahun	Kenema	Kono	Bombali	Kambia	Koinadugu	Port Loko	Tonkolili	Western	Total
1948–49	—	3	2	—	—	1	—	—	—	—	—	—	—	6
1949–50	1	8	2	11	1	4	—	—	1	—	1	—	—	29
1950–51	1	7	3	22	3	5	—	—	1	—	1	—	—	43
1951–52	1	9	4	22	15	5	—	—	2	—	2	—	1	61
1952–53	3	9	5	36	21	7	—	2	2	—	1	—	1	87
1953–54	5	11	15	44	46	8	—	1	2	—	1	—	2	135
1954–55	7	16	17	54	68	17	1	1	3	—	3	—	2	189
1955–56	8	19	32	54	74	31	1	1	3	—	6	1	2	232
1956–57	16	22	34	61	83	40	1	1	7	—	15	1	2	283
1957–58	6	22	29	46	86	52	7	1	12	—	19	8	3	291
1958–59	6	23	29	57	111	63	10	4	15	—	20	13	3	354
1959–60	13	26	30	72	126	76	15	5	23	1	20	16	4	427
1960–61	14	26	33	116	126	79	18	9	24	1	22	23	6	497
1961–62	29	71	34	125	141	87	19	11	34	1	27	35	15	629
1962–63	29	84	34	125	141	87	19	11	34	1	27	36	15	643
1963–64	58	99	34	126	144	87	19	11	43	1	28	40	16	706
1964–65	110	107	34	130	145	89	19	16	52	2	33	44	31	812
1965–66	151	120	53	130	145	89	19	16	56	2	38	52	35	906
1966–67	154	120	60	130	145	89	19	16	56	2	38	57	35	921

SOURCE: 1948–57 from Departmental Annual Reports; 1958–67 compiled by author from the Register of the Co-operative Department, Society Files, and from the Department's Black Book.

instigated locally by the people themselves, their chiefs, or their schoolteachers. However, because of the shortage of technical and supervisory personnel, the government was not able to appoint a Registrar of Co-operative Societies and actively encourage the movement until 1949.

The beginnings of the government-directed movement were, of necessity, small and localized. By the end of the first year of operations, six societies were under supervision—four of the previously initiated consumer societies as well as two pilot piassava-marketing organizations. From this base, the movement expanded almost without interruption.[51] Growth was continuous, as was areal expansion (Table 6). Spread effects were contagious, with existing societies acting as models for neighboring villages.

> A meeting of the best societies is almost like a revival meeting with members getting up to testify to their benefits. There seems something here that meets a felt need, and meets it by a process so simple that the most backward villagers may learn to understand it.[52]

The co-operative movement increased in intensity in the several core areas and gradually spread outward (Figure 17). Although the pattern of spread is quite complex, neighborhood effects are apparent. In reality the movement was not a simple homogeneous phenomenon. Rather, it was composed of several quite independent yet interacting parts. Although the general idea of co-operation diffused broadly, its acceptance was usually associated with one of several concrete examples. The ideas of piassava marketing seem to have had little relevance to the fishermen, and a consumer society usually did not act as a model for the cocoa farmer. Despite the fact that the earliest co-ops were formed in the north, the postwar expansion was largely in the south, and especially in Mende country. Acceptance or rejection reflected tribal differences and the fact of tribalism often acted as a barrier to its spread.[53]

51. Of the co-operative societies founded (approximately 1,050), 144 are now defunct because of financial difficulties, lack of interest among the members, new interests, dishonest officers removing funds, inaccessibility and difficulty of maintaining supervision, and because of drastic reductions in world prices for specific crops. The latter accounts for 37 closures of piassava-marketing societies in Pujehun District alone.

52. Sierra Leone, *Annual Report of the Department of Co-operation for the Year Ending 30th April 1954*, p. 1.

53. Johnson also cites the lack of response in the north to be due to the suspicious and independent-minded nature of the Temne peoples and the lack of interest of the chiefs and other big men, including one district commissioner. (R. E. Johnson, Ph.D. dissertation on the co-operative movement in Sierra Leone, in progress at Western Illinois University. Mr. Johnson kindly provided intermediate drafts of his section on "Areal Development.")

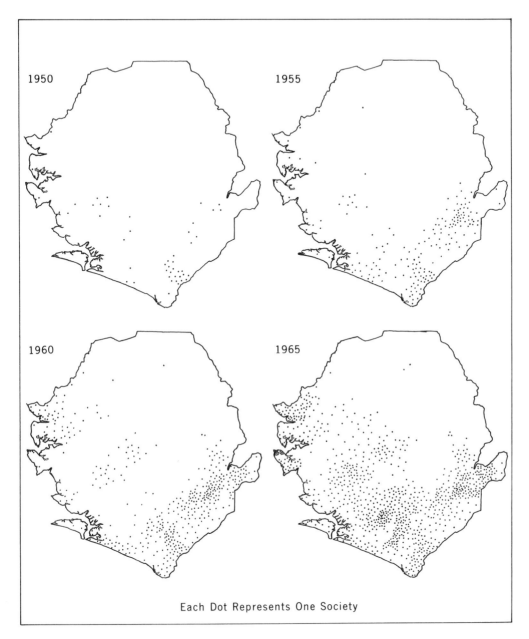

Figure 17.   Expansion of the Co-operative Movement

But the most important aspect was simple geographic proximity. The co-operative idea spread most rapidly to neighboring areas and was more readily adopted when the social and economic systems were compatible. The tendency was augmented by the explicit policy of the Co-operative Department to encourage and promote new societies to make the most efficient use of limited staff. Naturally the transport system was a vital determinant of nearness and access.

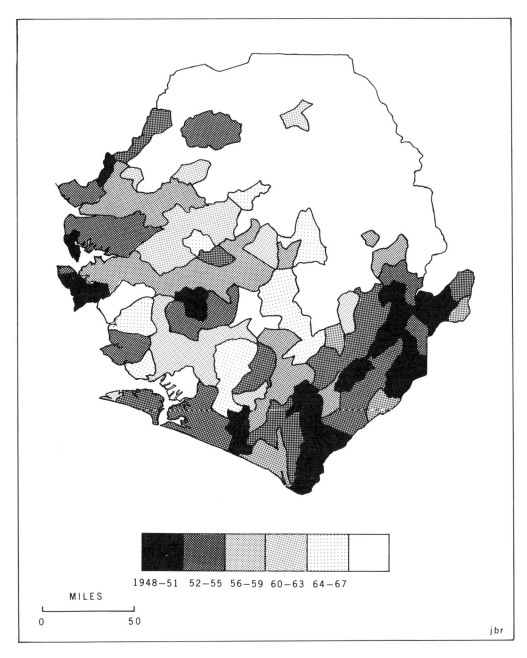

Figure 18.   Dates of Establishment of Co-operative Societies, by Chiefdom

From the original 6, well-dispersed societies formed in 1949, the number
rapidly expanded to 29 within a year. Much of the growth was due to the demonstration effect, especially in the piassava-marketing societies of Pujehun and
Bonthe. At the same time many other societies were formed in quite widely separated areas upon entirely different bases. Several new consumer societies de-

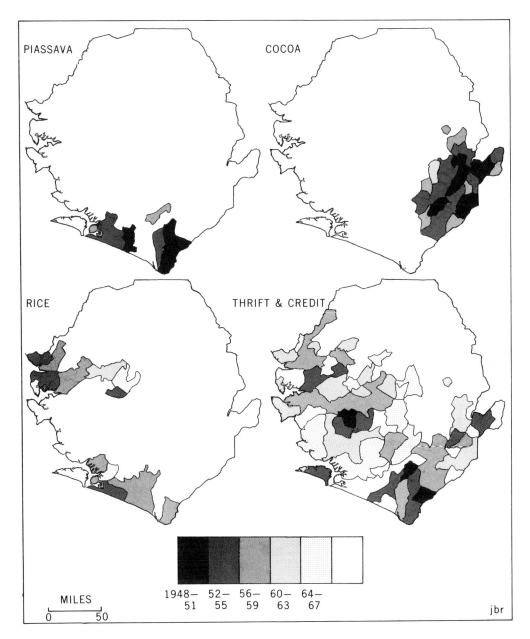

Figure 19.   Dates of Establishment of Co-operative Societies, by Type

veloped from pre-existing local efforts, and thrift and credit societies sprang up over wide areas, both from existing marketing societies and quite independently. Cocoa-marketing societies were formed in the Eastern Province, and in the early 1950's spread to the limits of cocoa production. Rice-producing co-ops, several employing new mechanical production techniques, were formed in Bonthe, Pujehun, Port Loko, and Kambia. Gradually, urban-based societies

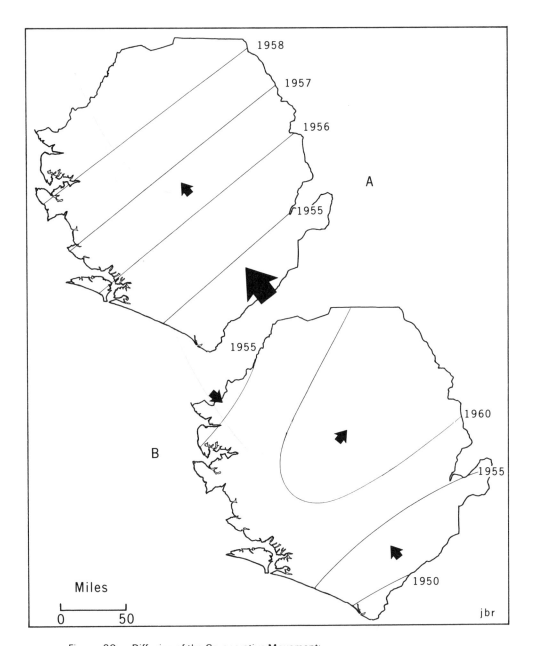

Figure 20.   Diffusion of the Co-operative Movement:
A—Linear Trend Surface; B—Quadratic Trend Surface

began to form as thrift and credit and consumer co-ops as well as several very specialized types—gara-dyeing, omole-marketing, and potmaking—in Freetown and the Western Area.

Much of the local detail of the process of diffusion may be removed by indexing the date at which the earliest society was founded in each chiefdom (Figure 18). Spatial-diffusion effects are visibly apparent, and the seeming complexity of the pattern is the result of the several separate types of societies interacting as they spread. However, the pattern can be decomposed into its component parts—cocoa, rice, etc.—each of which exhibits strong local diffusion patterns (Figure 19).

Further generalization of the diffusion process is produced by employing trend surface analysis as a high-pass filter to remove local anomalies and to highlight the general regional trends (Figure 20). The first linear surface differs radically from the previous examples and, rather than extending inland from the coast, depicts the influence of the early piassava and cocoa co-ops on the over-all spread from the south and east. Subsequent higher-order surfaces result in warpings of the trend to produce a horseshoe-like shape depicting the general spread inward, both south and east, from the coast. The pattern is quite distinct from the previous surfaces, and, rather than indexing a separate process, it provides an example of a diffusion process beginning within the rural areas rather than emanating from the capital.

POSTAL SERVICES

Vital to the political administration of the country and the commercial operations of the firms was the maintenance of a system of constant and efficient internal communications. Political control in the colonial period, to be effective, relied upon constant correspondence between the district officer handling immediate problems in the protectorate and the body of policy-making administrators in Freetown and London. The larger firms, as they established branches inland with the opening of the railway, depended upon continuous flows of information on prices, costs, and supplies. These vital services have been provided in large part by the network of post offices and postal agencies.

Postal services in Sierra Leone date from 1808 when the Freetown settlement was taken over by the British government as a crown colony. Service was at first confined to Freetown but was gradually extended to include the more important coastal trading stations such as Bonthe, York Island, Bendu, Sulima, and

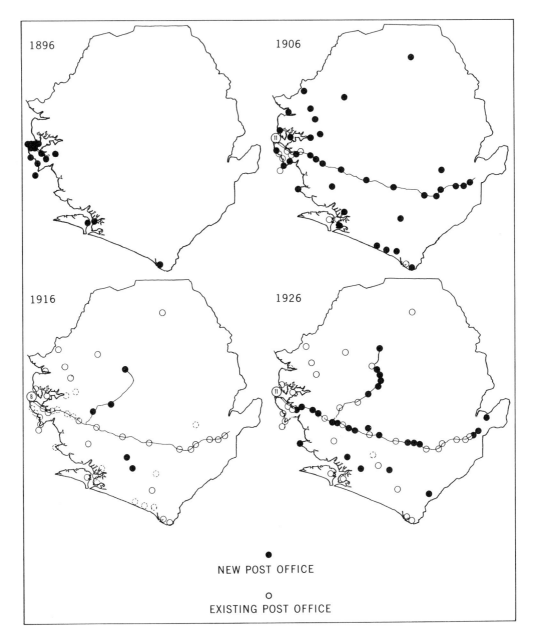

Figure 21.   Expansion of Postal Services, 1896 to 1926

Mano Salija. In 1892 the service was also expanded to many of the settler villages on the peninsula behind Freetown.

By 1896, at the declaration of the protectorate, postal communications were limited to Freetown, the villages, and a few coastal trading stations (Figure 21). Trading in the interior was largely in the hands of smaller middlemen, and political contact was limited to a few police posts; thus communications were not a vital issue in the interior.

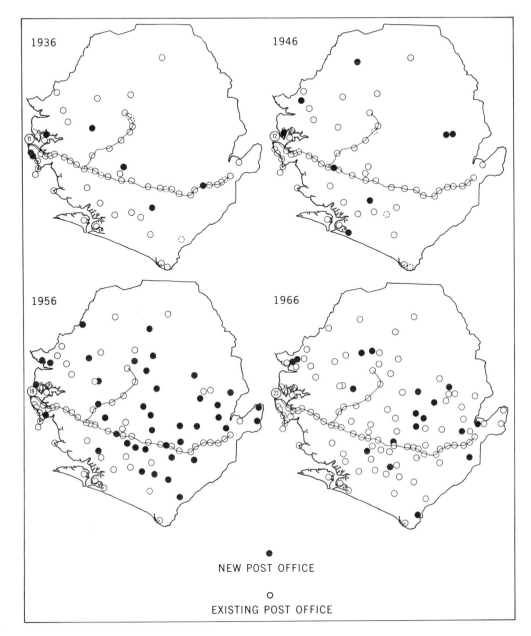

Figure 22.   Expansion of Postal Services, 1936 to 1966

With the expansion into the interior after 1896, post offices opened at the five newly established district headquarters and at several of the more important towns along the rail line. Other than for administration, the services were provided for the European mercantile community.

The pattern continued essentially unchanged for many years; the railway and the political headquarters remained the loci. The new additions to the network reflect the opening of the branch line, the alterations and additions to the system of district headquarters, and the new importance given to several inland towns by the construction of feeder roads. The railway served as the main carrier, with overland routes extending to several of the unconnected inland centers and launch services serving the coastal stations.

It was not until the 1950's that the factors determining the pattern, and the pattern itself, changed perceptibly (Figure 22). A more complete areal coverage began to emerge, partly as a result of the extension of road connections to most parts of the country, but also because of increased indigenous use of the mails with the expansion of co-operative marketing and the spread of education and the money economy. The more complete areal coverage also reflects a provision of infrastructure in preparation for independence. However, despite the wider areal coverage, the present-day pattern of postal facilities continues to reflect the influences of the past. The north-south differential is apparent and marks differences in literacy and commercial involvement as well as the influence of the railway on the provision of services in the south.

BANKING

Because of the traditional nature of Sierra Leone's economy, the demand for banking facilities has been severely restricted and highly localized. Prior to the 1950's, the banks served a limited segment of the population—the European administrative personnel, the large expatriate trading firms, the Lebanese traders, and the more prosperous members of the Creole community—residing in Freetown and a few protectorate towns. Gradually, as Sierra Leoneans have entered the money economy, the use of banks has greatly increased and the pattern of facilities, as a result, has greatly expanded. However, the demand for banking services still is limited, in part because their savings functions are replaced by the thrift and credit co-operative societies.

> In 1964 there were 430 such societies in both rural and urban areas, and they form the most important means of small-scale saving and credit for the majority of

Sierra Leoneans. These societies offer loans for expenses of cultivation and minor building as well as being a stimulus to regular saving.[54]

As a result, both the commercial banks and the Post Office Savings Banks are high-threshold functions occurring in only the larger towns or the more prosperous mining and agricultural areas.

The first savings bank was opened in 1882 at the Colonial Treasury, Freetown, and later, in 1895, a branch was established at Bonthe, an important trading center south along the coast. The first commercial bank in Freetown was opened by the Bank of British West Africa in 1894, and for administrative efficiency the Treasury Banks were transferred to the Post Office in 1896.[55] Gradually services were extended upcountry, first to Waterloo in 1901 and Moyamba in 1902. An ordinance was passed in 1903 extending the operations of the Post Office Savings Banks to the protectorate,[56] and during the same year branches were opened at each of the five district headquarters, with the respective district commissioners appointed as branch managers.[57] Later, other savings banks were opened in conjunction with the post office at several centers along the rail line. The banks were small and almost exclusively confined to small-scale savings.

With the opening of a branch agency at Bo in 1911, the Bank of British West Africa extended its operations into the protectorate. By the end of the decade further branches had been established at Bonthe, Blama, Kenema, Segbwema, and Pendembu, and Barclays Bank had begun operations in Freetown. Though both the government and commercial banks were able to coexist, the Post Office Savings Banks' business declined at many centers with the growth of the commercial banks.[58]

54. K. Swindell, in Clarke, *Sierra Leone in Maps*, p. 72.
55. Ordinance No. 30 of 1896.
56. Ordinance No. 5 of 1903.
57. *Sierra Leone Gazette*, January 28, 1904.
58. Great Britain, Colonial Office, *Colonial Report, 1920, Sierra Leone.* This was due to the very limited facilities offered by the Post Office Banks as compared to the full range of services available from the commercial banks. Also, it probably reflected the difficulty of withdrawing funds from the Post Office Banks.

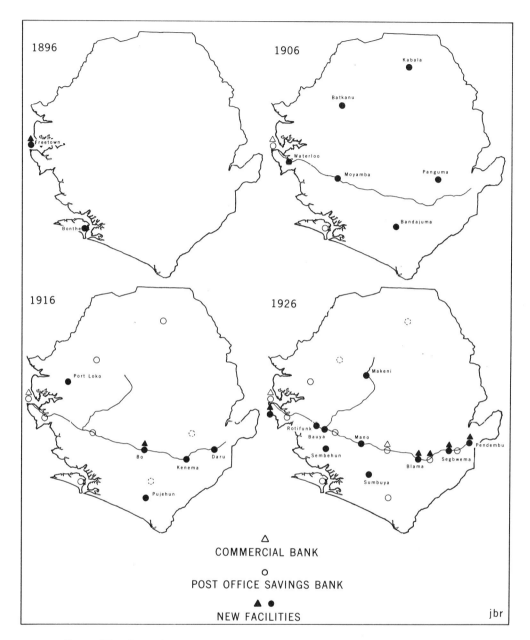

Figure 23.   Expansion of Banking Services, 1896 to 1926

The pattern remained essentially constant for some time, though further Post Office Savings Banks were opened along the rail line and at the new administrative centers. Because the government banks were operated as part of the post office, they were able to survive the depression years of the 1930's and, in fact, even extended their provision of facilities. The commercial banks were reduced in number by the stifling of trade (Figures 23 and 24).

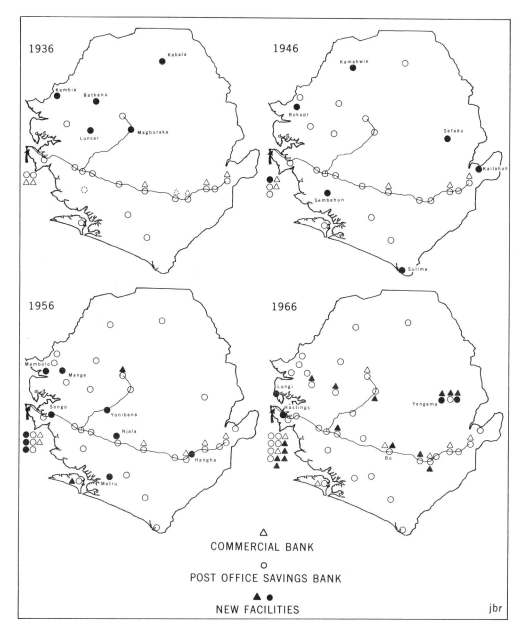

Figure 24.   Expansion of Banking Services, 1936 to 1966

With the lifting of the trade depression and the easing of wartime cutbacks, the pattern of banking facilities has expanded greatly. The new pattern reflects the spread of cash values away from the rail line, the boom economies of the mining areas, and the network of administrative centers and larger trading towns. Though the role of the Post Office Savings Banks also continues to expand, the commercial banks are assuming a larger and much more important role in the nation's banking. Their pattern reflects the major nodes of commercial activity, while the government banks also reflect an attempt to provide a wide areal coverage.

THE SPATIAL COMPONENTS OF MODERNIZATION

Further indices of modernization with locational coordinates are available, but their pattern and progress would appear to be remarkably similar to those already described. The extension of the telegraph system, with the exception of a few branches to administrative centers, followed the railway; the telephone network first extended along the rail line, though its services have since been extended over a much wider area; electricity has been provided to the provincial administrative centers.

It is evident from the description of the several elements of the modernization process that certain patterns recur again and again. Despite the fact that each of the indices has distinct origins, they all respond in their pattern of spread to the network of road and rail, to the urban-administrative hierarchy, and to the frictional effects of distance. Phrases such as "along the rail line," "up the roads," and "through the towns" were constantly repeated. Maps depicting the spread of such disparate indices as local political modernization (Figure 10) and educational facilities (Figure 15) have much in common. Despite the complexity of the modernization process, which involves changes in attitudes, behavior patterns, institutions, and infrastructure, there is an underlying spatial regularity. The indices and surrogates are interrelated and reinforce one another in their locational pattern. The overriding fabric—the transportation network and the urban-administrative hierarchy—directs and determines the pattern of spatial evolution.

Many of the surrogates of modernization are similar because they represent colonial administrative policy and machinery. It was no accident that all the early hospitals, post offices, and banks opened in the administrative headquarters. Yet many of the other manifestations of modernization were quite independent of the administration. The commercial banks were located by considerations distinct from those affecting the Post Office Banks. Schools were opened by competing

TABLE 7.   MODERNIZATION VARIABLES

No.	Name	Description
1	DATESCHOOL	Date of establishment of the first primary school in the chiefdom
2	DATEHEALTH	Date of opening of the first health facility
3	DATEHOSPIT	Date of opening of a permanent hospital facility
4	DATESECSCH	Date of opening of the chiefdom's first secondary school
5	DATEPOST	Date of establishment of postal services
6	DATEBANK	Date of opening of first bank
7	DATETELEP	Date of establishment of telephone link
8	DATETELEG	Date of establishment of telegraph link
9	DATETRANS	Date at which chiefdom was linked with the national transport network
10	D.H.Q.	Dummy variable weighted by the number of years of having a district, provincial ($\times 2$), or protectorate ($\times 3$) H.Q.
11	DATEN.A.	Date of establishment of Native Administration form of chiefdom government
12	EDUCAT	Per cent attending school, 1963
13	LITER	Per cent literate in English, 1963
14	URBGROW	Absolute increase in urban population from 1927 to 1963
15	URBPERCENT	Per cent of chiefdom population residing in places over 2,000, 1963
16	TRADITION	Per cent of labor force engaged in farming, fishing, and hunting, 1963
17	ROADDEN	Miles of road per square mile of chiefdom area, 1963
18	LGTOWN	Absolute size of largest urban place in chiefdom, 1963
19	NONMOBILE	Per cent of population residing in chiefdom, born elsewhere, 1963
20	OUTMIG	Per capita rate of migration to Freetown, 1963
21	DATEELEC	Date of installation of electricity supply
22	DATECOOP	Date of opening of first co-operative society

mission societies. The co-operative movement spread under its own momentum, guided only slightly by administrative policies.

To determine the degree of spatial regularity of the modernization process and to provide a general index of its pattern, a set of status variables indicating the areal variation of measures of education, literacy, immobility, migration rates, urbanization, road density, traditional employment, and administrative function have been added to the previously discussed set of process variables. Together, the

TABLE 8. Matrix of Correlation Coefficients (decimal points omitted)

Var.	2	3	4	5	6	7	8	9	10	11	12	13	14	15	16	17	18	19	20	21	22
1	21	34	47	44	43	44	59	63	-46	58	-65	-71	-46	-40	24	-44	-48	41	-49	37	22
2		35	33	44	40	35	30	31	-23	31	-16	-19	-15	-19	21	-10	-13	-01	-14	23	13
3			65	38	68	68	46	38	-59	32	-42	-45	-40	-51	39	-23	-34	25	-32	63	23
4				43	56	49	44	43	-47	36	-42	-46	-33	-43	26	-20	-29	27	-27	60	22
5					47	38	41	54	-26	37	-31	-32	-25	-38	17	-11	-18	38	-15	34	23
6						84	66	48	-51	33	-46	-49	-30	-45	31	-19	-28	26	-29	58	27
7							72	53	-53	39	-49	-51	-31	-46	33	-21	-30	29	-31	67	30
8								60	-40	38	-48	-46	-24	-31	16	-18	-24	27	-26	44	27
9									-45	57	-49	-58	-45	-37	38	-43	-45	27	-47	38	38
10										-48	54	67	77	66	-49	71	78	-28	76	-64	-18
11											-50	-58	-57	-35	21	-62	-61	17	-63	33	29
12												86	48	46	-13	47	51	-48	48	-51	-33
13													73	63	-42	66	74	-54	68	-54	-21
14														73	-53	90	97	-39	88	-34	-05
15															-51	47	63	-61	53	-46	-08
16																-43	-50	06	-49	33	-08
17																	96	-16	97	-26	-08
18																		-29	95	-32	-07
19																			-15	24	17
20																				-34	-09
21																					25

22 variables index the existing levels of modernization and the historic growth processes (Table 7). No one is unique in itself, nor are there any perfect associations (Table 8). The correlation coefficients indicate a high degree of interrelatedness among certain groups of variables, while others are weakly associated to the clusters and yet other variables are quite independent.

Although it is not geometrically possible to portray the interrelations among the 22 variables, the correlation matrix performs the same function algebraically. The association of the variables may be conceived of as a scattering of points in a space of 22 dimensions. The scattering can take on any of a large number of shapes, depending upon the associations and clusterings of the variables. In the limit, if each variable were independent of all others, the shape of the scatter would be circular. Because there are associations or correlations among the variables, the points tend to cluster and take on an ellipsoidal shape. Those variables grouped about the major axis of the ellipse form the most dominant grouping and, in terms of principal-components analysis, form the first component or axis. Such a components analysis has been employed in the search for the dimensions of modernization and to determine the degree to which the several phenomena have a single overriding pattern of response to the nation's spatial fabric (Table 9).

Five components were derived, accounting for 76.8 per cent of the total variance of the original data matrix.[59] The factor loadings indicate the degree to which each of the variables is associated with each of the factors. The modernization process in Sierra Leone does have a strong overriding common dimension. The first factor accounts for 45.5 per cent of the variance and is composed of high and roughly equal loadings from most of the 22 variables; only the evolution of the co-operative movement and the spread of health facilities are distinctly separate. Thus the major component forms an excellent summary measure composed of weighted contributions of the original variables. A mapping of the scores of the first component indicates a very marked difference between Freetown and the provinces, with the Western Area assuming an intermediate position

59. Factor extraction was terminated when eigenvalues of less than 1 were obtained.

TABLE 9.   MODERNIZATION FACTOR LOADINGS

Variable	F_1	F_2	F_3	F_4	F_5
DATESCHOOL	.72	.09	−.41	.05	.09
DATEHEALTH	.36	.33	.21	.45	.41
DATEHOSPIT	.67	.35	.39	−.09	−.11
DATESECSCH	.63	.37	.16	−.05	−.01
DATEPOST	.51	.41	−.14	.08	.56
DATEBANK	.68	.50	.21	.02	−.09
DATETELEP	.71	.48	.18	.01	−.20
DATETELEG	.62	.46	−.14	.13	−.09
DATETRANS	.72	.17	−.25	.29	.15
D.H.Q.	−.83	.20	−.24	.03	.18
DATEN.A.	.69	−.13	−.28	.39	.02
EDUCAT	−.73	−.06	.38	.19	.21
LITER	−.88	.14	.21	.18	.06
URBGROW	−.80	.53	−.07	.07	−.10
URBPERCENT	−.73	.12	−.18	.43	−.25
TRADITION	.52	−.21	.52	.04	.21
ROADDEN	−.71	.64	.04	−.18	.07
LGTOWN	−.79	.58	−.03	−.05	.01
NONMOBILE	.47	.08	−.34	−.69	.28
OUTMIG	−.77	.56	−.03	−.19	.09
DATEELEC	.67	.31	.26	−.14	−.30
DATECOOP	.30	.32	−.40	.16	−.31
Eigenvalue	10.00	2.96	1.54	1.32	1.06
Percentage of variance	45.5	13.5	7.0	6.0	4.8

between the two (Figure 25). The areal pattern of modernization in the provinces is not a smooth, even surface, nor does it indicate a regular decline in levels of modernization with distance away from Freetown. Rather, it depicts a generally low surface with local peaks associated with the centers of the urban-administrative hierarchy, a marked north-south differential, and a linear wedge of higher values associated with the rail line. It is evident that this first General Modernization component does reflect the fabric as defined by the network and the hierarchy.

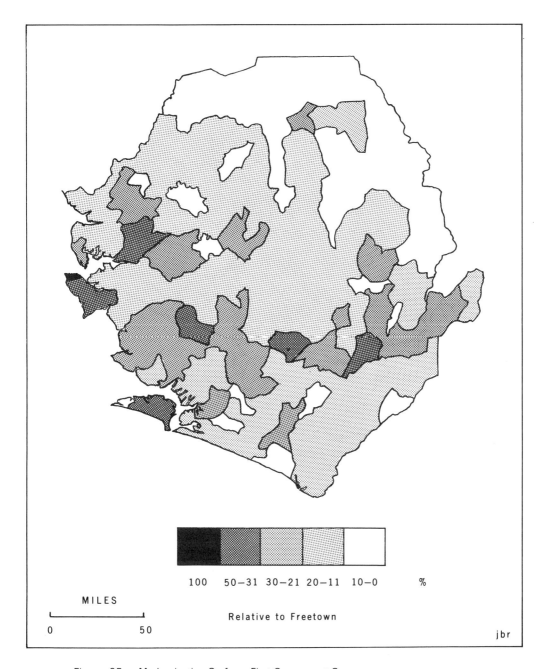

Figure 25. Modernization Surface: First Component Scores

To filter the spatial regularity from the general pattern of modernization, trend surface analysis has been employed. The first-order surface indicates a progression of modernization levels increasing inland from the coast, and subsequent higher-order surfaces indicate a warping of the east-west trend to incorporate the effects of the wedge of development associated with the rail line and to indicate the

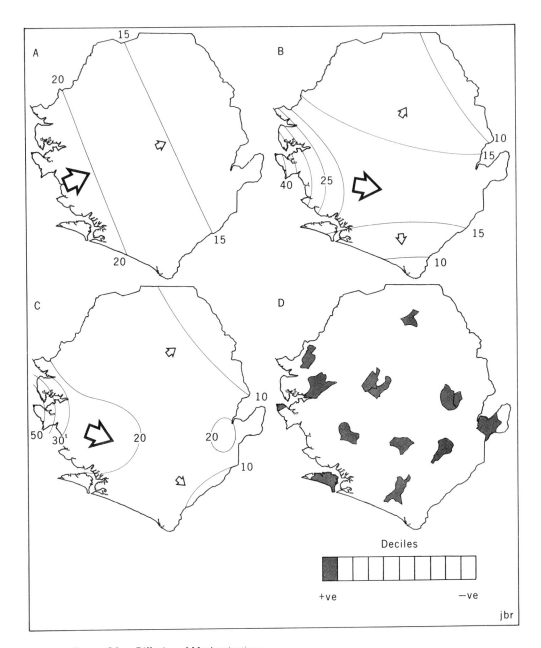

Figure 26.   Diffusion of Modernization:
A—Linear Trend Surface; B—Quartic Trend Surface; C—Sixth-Order Trend
Surface; D—High Positive Residuals from Sixth-Order Surface

strong distance-decay function from Freetown inland. Even after the derivation of
the sixth-order surface, the strength of the urban-administrative hierarchy is
evident in the map of residuals (Figure 26). Thus it is evident that the process of
modernization, as summarized by the components analysis, is dominated and

directed by the network and the hierarchy, which together define the spatial fabric of the country.[60]

60. Subsequent components are described in Table 9. Despite the fact that together the four components account for 31.3 per cent of the variance of the original data matrix, they are unimportant when compared to the first component and define certain more specific combinations of the modernization indices.

Response: Migration to Freetown

According to the chief, very many young men go off to Freetown on the lorries, returning home after a while to boast about life in Freetown; then they disappear again, drawing many of their age mates after them.[1]

From the preceding chapters it is clear that the recent history of Sierra Leone has been characterized by dramatic change. The evolution of an urban-administrative hierarchy and the spread of a network of road and rail have structured geographic space, while the diffusion of schools, co-operatives, and post offices has brought modern institutions. However, the transition has not only been characterized by alterations and extensions of infrastructure and social services but has extended even to the very core of the social system, affecting attitudes and behavior patterns and resulting in new ways of life and extensions of human areal horizons. New roads, new schools, the opening of post offices and dispensaries—all have resulted not only in improved local conditions, but in the restructuring and re-evaluation of the geographic space in which men live their daily lives. The school has brought new ideas; the road, new paths of movement; the post office, new contacts with the outside world.

Perhaps the most dramatic change is the evolution of an urban system, providing not only a new environment but also a new focus of economic activity. Within such an evolving central place structure, new markets open, a new value system diffuses, and traditional ties are weakened. Prior to European contact, true urban centers did not exist. Although some villages were larger than others because of the power of strong chiefs or better agricultural land, the traditional pattern of life and settlement was rural and agricultural. Contact with the external world, with its concomitant stimulation of trade, caused a partial reorganization of geographic space. Certain towns grew in importance as trading centers—especially at ports, heads of navigation, and along the road and rail network—and as administrative centers.[2] Totally new functions were added to the towns as

1. M. Banton, *West African City* (London: Oxford University Press, 1957), p. 53.
2. M. E. E. Harvey, "A Geographical Study of the Pattern, Processes and Consequences of Urban Growth in Sierra Leone in the Twentieth Century" (Ph.D. diss., University of Durham, 1966).

TABLE 10.   URBAN GROWTH IN SIERRA LEONE

Center	1927 Population	1963 Population
Freetown	73,126	157,613
Bo	3,780	26,613
Kenema	1,200	13,246
Makeni	1,000	12,304
Lunsar	78	12,132
Koidu	96	11,706
Yengema	144	7,313
Magburaka	348	6,371
Segbwema	2,790	6,258
Bonthe	5,400	6,230
Jaiama NY	864	6,064
Port Loko	2,700	5,809
Yomandu	978	5,469
Kailahun	2,772	5,419
Barma	360	5,280
Blama	1,812	5,073

SOURCE: 1927 data from M. E. E. Harvey, "A Geographical Study of the Pattern, Processes and Consequences of Urban Growth in Sierra Leone in the Twentieth Century" (Ph.D. diss., University of Durham, 1966); 1963 data from *1963 Population Census of Sierra Leone,* Vol. I, Table 6.

they became the loci of wage employment, and with the growth of cash incomes people began to acquire radically new ways of life. They also began to move as they had never moved before, not only to the towns in the near vicinity but often to towns traditionally associated with other tribes. The administrative towns, and especially Freetown, the capital, became the magnet for mass seasonal and permanent moves.

A system of towns grew at the district headquarters, along the rail line, at the heads of navigation, and in the mining areas. Rates of increase were enormous as most of the new towns grew from small village origins in a few years. Yet in terms of sheer absolute numbers, the intensity of growth at Freetown was unmatched (Table 10). With its dominant administrative and trade role, Freetown became increasingly prominent, exhibiting the primacy typical of capitals in many underdeveloped areas.[3]

The tempo of movement increased within the rural sphere as well. With the imposition of stability and law and order by the colonial power, people could move beyond their village, chiefdom, or tribe without fear of enslavement or harm. Documentation of the movement is difficult, as historical records of rural population are simply not available, but the general pattern of movement can be depicted by a mapping of the population residing in each chiefdom which was born elsewhere (Figure 27). The influx of migrants into the diamond areas is pronounced, as is the movement into the chiefdoms with urban centers and along the rail route, but everywhere there is evidence of movement, even in the most isolated areas.

Migration is far from being a recent phenomenon in Sierra Leone or Africa; evidence of the movement of peoples dates to the earliest records.[4] Yet the colonial situation radically altered the scope and scale. It has meant the removal of some restraints and the imposition of new foci. The provision of law and order, the extension of easy routes of travel, and the location of new towns with the possibility of wage employment and freedom from traditional restrictions effectively reordered the pattern of movement.

THE STUDY OF MIGRATION

Although the history of the study of migration can be traced far back in the annals of inquiry, systematic analysis may be said to date from the late nineteenth cen-

3. M. Jefferson, "The Law of Primate Cities," *Geographical Review*, XXIX (1939), 226–32; B. J. L. Berry, "City Size Distribution and Economic Development," *Economic Development and Cultural Change*, IX (1961), 573–88.

4. I. Wallerstein, "Migration in West Africa: The Political Perspective," in *Urbanization and Migration in West Africa*, ed. H. Kuper (Berkeley: University of California Press, 1965), pp. 148–59.

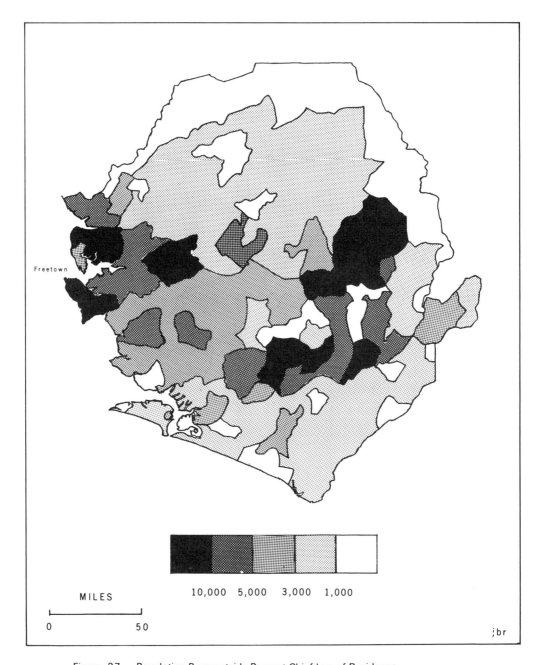

Figure 27.   Population Born outside Present Chiefdom of Residence

tury and Ravenstein's "Laws of Migration."[5] Studying the flow of migrants to Paris, he indicated that their movements were related inversely to the distance from Paris and directly to the size of the community from which the migrants orig-

5. E. G. Ravenstein, "The Laws of Migration," *Journal of the Royal Statistical Society,* XLVIII (1885), 167–227; LII (1889), 241–301.

inated, thereby producing the first expression of a gravity-type formulation fitting the behavior of human masses. The notion of a "law" of human interaction lay dormant for many years until it was revived by Reilly, who used a similar notion of attraction of mass and friction of distance in the study of trading areas of urban centers.[6] However, it was not until the early 1940's that the notion of a general law of migration began to gain respectability in the social sciences. G. K. Zipf reintroduced the notion as an empirical reality;[7] Stouffer deduced the logically similar though circular intervening-opportunity model;[8] and J. Q. Stewart, a physicist, drew the analogies of gravitation and potential and applied them to human behavior.[9] The basic tenet underlying these formulations has been that migration, rather than being a unique phenomenon confined to specific geographic areas and populations, was general and could be described in terms of lawlike statements incorporating a few simple variables.

Subsequent studies have tended to support the findings of Zipf, Stouffer, and Stewart,[10] while further refining the understanding of the mechanism of human migration. Hagerstrand has shown the feedback effects between migration and information flow,[11] and the thesis of a stepwise migration process operating through the urban hierarchy has been developed and substantiated.[12] These

6. W. J. Reilly, "Methods for the Study of Retail Relationships," *University of Texas Bulletin*, No. 2944 (1929).

7. G. K. Zipf, *Human Behavior and the Principle of Least Effort* (Reading, Mass.: Addison-Wesley, 1949).

8. S. A. Stouffer, "Intervening Opportunities: A Theory Relating Mobility and Distance," *American Sociological Review*, V (1940), 845–67.

9. J. Q. Stewart, "A Measure of the Influence of a Population at a Distance," *Sociometry*, V (1952), 63–71; and Stewart, "The Development of Social Physics," *American Journal of Physics*, XVIII (1950), 239–53.

10. See the numerous examples cited in G. Olsson, *Distance and Human Interaction: A Review and Bibliography* (Philadelphia: Regional Science Research Institute, 1965).

11. T. Hagerstrand, "Migration and Area," in *Migration in Sweden: A Symposium, Lund Studies in Geography*, ser. B, Human Geography, XIII (1957), 27–158.

12. G. Olsson, "Distance and Human Interaction: A Migration Study," *Geografiska Annaler*, ser. B, XLVII (1965), 3–43; and Hagerstrand, "Migration and Area."

studies have all indicated the supreme importance of economic factors. Distance, as measured in time, miles, or dollars, has proved to be the most consistently important variable,[13] while income, employment, information, housing, and intervening opportunities have also been found vital to the understanding of such movements.

Thus, the study of migration and its causes in Europe and Anglo-America has focused largely on inductive generalization, quantitative model construction, and attempts at testing hypotheses and prototheories. In contrast, African migration research has emphasized unique studies in specific temporal, geographic, and methodological contexts, seldom seeking general and comparative relationships; irrationality and interpersonal and intertribal differences were seen as preventing general statements from being formulated, and the lack of hard quantitative data precluded attempts at model-building. It was argued that the African migrant was not acting solely in response to economic forces; that he continued to be drawn to the bright lights of the cities despite poor housing and lack of job opportunities, while economic and social improvements in the rural home areas seem to have acted as a stimulus to urban migration. Further, prominent Africanists have criticized model-building and theory-testing in African studies because it is said that the assumptions used in the social sciences and economics are of relevance only to Western societies.[14]

It is in the light of the findings of the Western migration studies, and with an appreciation of the African situation, that the study of the pattern of migration to Freetown, the capital of Sierra Leone, is undertaken. A descriptive linear model is constructed, based upon empirical data of unusually fine areal detail. The induc-

13. J. B. Riddell, "Toward an Understanding of the Friction of Distance" (M.A. thesis, University of Toronto, 1965), chap. 1.

14. M. J. Herskovits, "Special Problems in Underdeveloped Countries: Discussion," *American Economic Review,* XLIV (1959), 200. The position is quite valid in terms of purely deductive economic theory, as primitive and peasant economies are instituted quite differently from the market-permeated Western societies upon which most of economic theory is based. However, this should not exclude inductive generalization at present nor future deductive formulation specific to the underdeveloped world.

tive generalization relates migration to a set of explanatory variables and shows migration to be a response to the complex structuring of geographic space and the diffusion of modernization.[15]

THE GROWTH OF FREETOWN

Almost from its inception as a settlement of freed slaves in 1787, Freetown has been unrivaled in Sierra Leone for its supremacy, not only in terms of sheer num-

TABLE 11.   FREETOWN: POPULATION COMPOSITION

	1901		1963	
	Number	Percentage	Number	Percentage
Creole	16,505	47.9	27,730	21.7
Temne	4,494	13.0	30,595	23.9
Mende	2,291	6.6	12,561	9.8
Limba	1,423	4.1	18,410	14.4
Kroo	1,903	5.5	4,461	3.5
Loko	198	0.6	5,842	4.6
Susu	1,417	4.1	3,865	3.0
Mandinka	1,037	3.0	3,141	2.4
Fulani	270	0.8	6,533	5.1
Others	4,925	14.3	14,779	11.6
Total	34,463	99.9	127,917	100.0

SOURCE: 1901 data derived from M. Banton, *West African City* (London: Oxford University Press, 1957); 1963 data from *1963 Population Census of Sierra Leone,* Vol. II, Table 3.

bers but also as an economic, administrative, and educational center. Its early growth resulted largely from the freeing of slaves recaptured by the British navy

15. The only other model-formulation approach to the study of African migration is that of the Northwestern team. However, because of the gross areal aggregation of their data base, the study has little geographic relevance. See R. E. Beals, M. B. Levy, C. F. Menezes, and L. N. Moses, *Labor Migration and Regional Development in Ghana* (Report of the Transportation Center, Northwestern University, January, 1966).

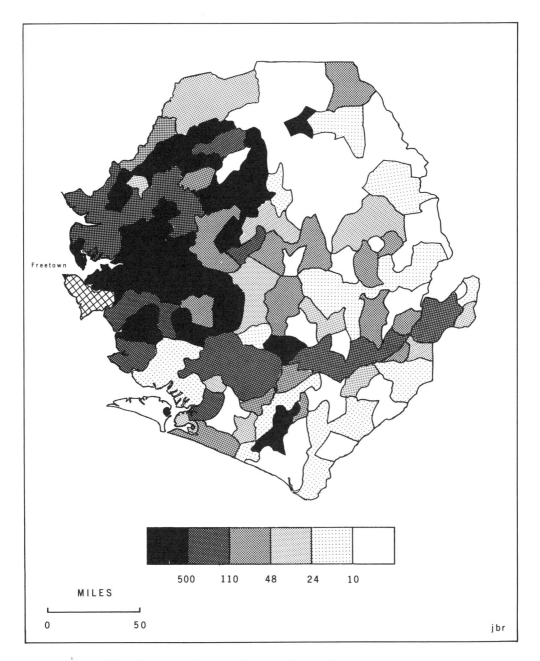

Figure 28.   Birthplace of Freetown Residents Born in Provinces

operating from the Freetown estuary. Almost 74,000 persons were rescued from
the slave ships bound for the Americas in the period 1808 to 1877. All were landed
at Freetown, although later some returned to their homelands. Many settled in the
villages on the colony peninsula behind Freetown, but those remaining in Freetown caused a steady increase in size. By 1833 Freetown had a population of 9,937,

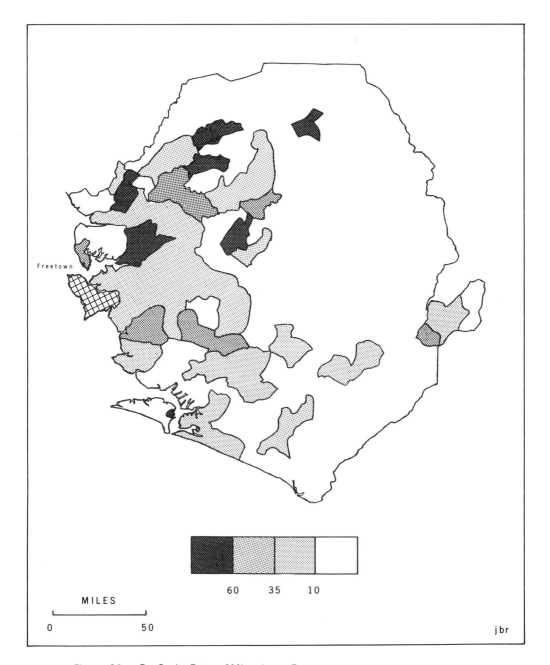

Figure 29.   Per Capita Rates of Migration to Freetown

and by 1848 the figure had almost doubled to 18,190.[16]

As it increased in size, Freetown increased in attractiveness to the peoples of the hinterland. By 1891 the population had risen to over 30,000, yet descendants

16. Banton, *West African City*, p. 4. For a detailed history of the early days of the colony, see C. Fyfe, *A History of Sierra Leone* (London: Oxford University Press, 1962).

of the freed slaves constitituted only slightly over half of the inhabitants.[17] Precise data on the origins of the migrants at that time are unavailable, but the dominant non-Creole groups included tribes from the immediate hinterland (Mende, Temne, and Limba), those groups traditionally associated with trade in the interior (Mandinka and Fulani), and the seafaring Kroo from Liberia. Of these, the Temnes were dominant, comprising just under 10 per cent of the total population. The early importance of the migrant groups in Freetown life is confirmed by the fact that as early as the 1880's tribal headmen were officially recognized in Freetown,[18] and complaints began to appear in the local press that the newcomers were creating serious social problems.[19]

By 1901 the Creoles had lost their majority in the Freetown population and, by 1963, their plurality (Table 11). Despite the fact that their numbers had nearly doubled in the 62-year period, they were beginning to be swamped by the relatively mass migration of the hinterland peoples, especially from the Temne, Limba, Mende, Fulani, and Loko tribes. In addition to being the capital and the traditional heart of Creole culture, Freetown has become the largest Temne town, the largest Mende town, and the largest Limba town!

THE MIGRATION PATTERN AND SOME HYPOTHESES

The analysis of the migration to Freetown employed the unpublished records of the *1963 Population Census of Sierra Leone* to obtain a measure of the origins of the Freetown population.[20] Among the questions asked the residents was the place of birth, by chiefdom, if born outside the Western Area. Of the 96,059 satisfactory responses, a little over one-third (33,706) were born in the provinces. Their origins are diverse and include all but four of the chiefdoms (Figure 28).

17. A. T. Porter, *Creoledom* (London: Oxford University Press, 1963).

18. M. Banton, "Tribal Headmen in Freetown," *Journal of African Administration,* VI (1954), 140–44.

19. Porter, *Creoledom,* p. 62.

20. This information was kindly supplied by the Central Statistics Office, Freetown.

The raw data have been standardized by the population of the chiefdom of origin to produce per capita rates of migration as a measure of levels of response to the historical process of change (Figure 29). The areal pattern of variation is most suggestive in the search for clues to the complex process involved in migration to the capital city. A distance-decay effect is most apparent, with migration rates generally decreasing with distance from Freetown. The influence of the major lines of transportation is obvious from a cursory inspection of the map, as a linear pattern of high values extends west-east to coincide with the location of the rail line. Similarly, the effects of the larger provincial towns are apparent, with the larger centers, especially the district headquarters, generating higher rates of migration than the surrounding rural areas. The effects of land hunger in some of the Bombali chiefdoms also seems to be evident, together with the influence of the diamond-mining areas as intervening opportunities reducing the rate of movement to the capital.

In all the numerous writings on migration in Africa, no consistent set of conclusions has appeared—nor, in fact, has generality often been sought.[21] Usually the findings stand in splendid isolation from one another, and, even if reference is made to other findings, the methods and data are so divergent as to provide no meaningful comparisons. Numerous explanations of the process of urban migration have been put forth. At times they are assumed to operate independently, at other times, in combination. The most frequently cited include:

Forces operating within the home area:
1. Deterioration in traditional subsistence agriculture, often resulting in a reduced carrying capacity of the land. Hunger and starvation are the results. The deterioration is usually associated with population increases, with resultant increased soil erosion and insufficient fallow periods between plantings.
2. Hazards, such as drought, flood, and pest.

21. Kuper, *Urbanization and Migration in West Africa;* and R. P. Simms, *Urbanization in West Africa: A Review of Current Literature* (Evanston, Ill.: Northwestern University Press, 1965).

3. Fear of witchcraft.

4. A desire by many, especially the young, to break from traditional authority and discipline.

5. Need for cash to pay taxes or brideprice or to buy some of the new goods available.

6. New aspirations, often created by local schools, which cannot be satisfied in tribal society.

7. Migration to the city as a part of the initiation rite. Anthropologists have found in some areas and societies that men are not considered eligible for marriage until they have spent a period of time away from home.

Urban attractions:

1. The prestige associated with urban employment.

2. The possibility of earning wages and attaining a higher standard of living.

3. The educational advantages of the city.

4. The psychological attraction of the city, with its bright lights, leisure activities, numerous shops, and large crowds.

5. The lack of traditional restrictions in the urban place.

Between:

1. New and better roads, so that the city has become closer in terms of time, distance, cost, or energy exerted.

2. The availability of relatively cheap transport with the increased use of trucks.

3. The lures of labor recruiters.

4. The imposition of law and order. The "stranger" has less to fear in moving through or living in lands of other tribes.

5. The circular and cumulative feedback effect. Once some members of a village move to the city, others become less hesitant to make the move because it is less of a break with the traditional group. More

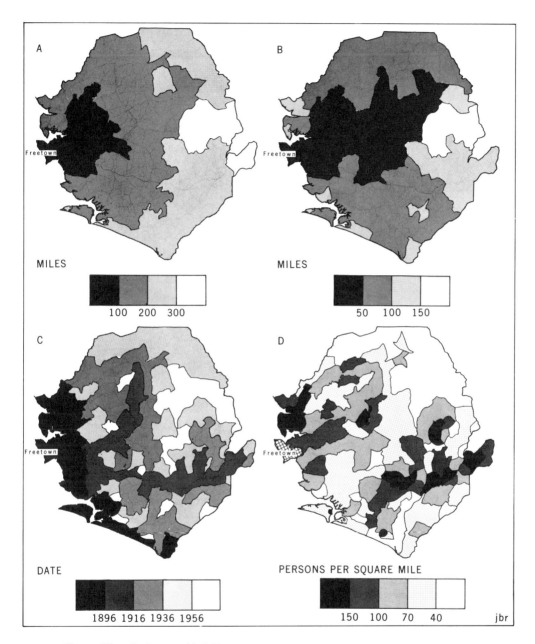

Figure 30. Explanatory Variables:
A—Road Distance to Freetown; B—Relative Inaccessibility; C—Date Connected to Transport System; D—Population Density

information is also available on employment opportunities and the freedom of urban life.

Based on the above suggestions and the inferences which can be drawn from an examination of the mapping of per capita rates of migration to Freetown, a set of explanatory variables might be posited whose areal variation will lead to a descriptive model of the migration process. Naturally, it is assumed that no one variable is sufficient to explain the complex process, nor is it supposed that all variables act with the same intensity throughout the population.

Distance

The most apparent factor to a geographer is that of distance effects. These have been shown to be the most consistently important variable in the explanation of European and Anglo-American migration patterns, and, if the findings on the changes in the frictional effects of distance over time with transport improvements have cross-cultural reference, we may expect distance effects to be even stronger in the African situation. Distance measures roughly the cost of movement, or the energy and time involved. It is also partially a psychological factor, for it is a surrogate measure of social distance in the sense that language differences, food and dietary habits, social practices, and the quality and quantity of information available have a high probability of being accentuated by physical distance.

The concept of distance is simple, but its effects and measurement are rather more complex. Distance can be measured in terms of road distance, relative isolation or inaccessibility,[22] and by the date at which improved means of transportation become available to link the area with the city and the wider world (Figure 30). Each of these measures a specific quality of distance and all are employed in the initial analysis. Migration is hypothesized to be inversely proportional to distance in its several gauges.

Population

The larger the number of people, the greater the potential number of migrants. We could expect such a relationship to be true for Sierra Leone, although it is highly

22. Inaccessibility was operationally defined as the absolute difference between road distance and air distance from the main settlement of each chiefdom to Freetown.

complicated by the intricate and varying relationship between man and the land. Unfortunately, data do not exist for measuring the land base, and an attempt has been made to measure the effects of population pressure, employing the rather crude surrogate of population density (Figure 30). A positive relationship is hypothesized between migration rates and population density, but the relationship is not expected to be precise because of the difficulty of accounting for carrying capacity and population pressure.

Education

Perhaps one of the most perplexing developmental questions is the role of education in affecting change. In a sense, it depends upon the quality of the education. If it provides the means to enhance traditional ways by improving agricultural techniques, introducing basic marketing and business principles, and emphasizing local community development, then education can be conservative and retard the outflow of people from rural areas. However, in general, education tends to introduce a wider world and to break down the traditional ties to the family and the tribe. The educated person has a wider knowledge of opportunities available to him, and the skills he has acquired in the education process make more and better jobs open to him.

It is hypothesized that in Sierra Leone, because of differing levels and attitudes toward education, the effects of education on migration should vary from one part of the country to another. Though not ubiquitous, educational opportunities have been widespread in the southern half of the country, where the Christian missions and their schools were rapidly accepted by the people. However, in the north, the Muslim people largely rejected the missions and their schools, with the result that the general level of Western education has been much lower and attitudes to it quite different.

Education is difficult to measure, as it is a continuous process, usually begun formally but often continuing throughout the individual's lifetime. Hence, the effects of several measures are considered. The percentage of school-age children attending school measures the quantity of the present educational system, though not the quality (see Figure 32). Long-term effects are reflected in literacy rates and by the date at which formal education was first established in the area (Figure 13). All are hypothesized to be positively associated with migration, although distinct northern and southern regional effects are expected.

Urbanization

Little has been published about the effects of the small provincial centers on the pattern of migration to the city. It might be contended that they offer an alternative to a long-distance move to the city, and certainly they have experienced rapid growth (Table 10). However, it is hypothesized that these towns, rather than acting as alternatives, fulfill the role of catalysts, introducing people to urban attitudes, skills, and ways of life which prepare them or their descendants for the move to the city. In effect, they smooth the transition from rural to city life by providing a quasi-urban environment in close physical proximity to the local tribe. A stepwise migration process is thus posited with persons moving from the rural areas to the growing provincial towns. At such centers they acquire urban ways, and later they move on to Freetown.

At the chiefdom level, urbanization can be measured in several ways, each defining part of the essence of the urban influence. Tertiary employment data have been used to measure job opportunities in the provincial towns, and the percentage of the chiefdom population residing in centers of over 2,000 provides a measure of the local importance of the urban centers. The absolute size of the largest urban place in the chiefdom measures the intensity of the local urban effects, and urban growth as measured by the absolute growth of urban centers between 1927 and 1963 indicates areas of increasing urbanization.[23] Because of the large relative importance of the district headquarters towns, with their cluster of administrative functions and the concomitant location of key services such as hospitals, banks, post offices, and secondary schools, a binary variable was also included in the analysis to indicate the presence or absence of a district headquarters in a chief-

23. The data are from Harvey, "Geographical Study."

dom (Figures 31 and 32). It is hypothesized that any and all of these urban variables will be strongly associated with levels of migration to Freetown.

Traditional Sector

The concept of tradition is also difficult to define and measure, but as it was considered to be an important variable in explaining the movement of people, it has
been included in the analysis. In essence, it is assumed to have the opposite effect
of the urban variables, and is measured in both economic and political terms.
Economically, the percentage of the chiefdom population engaged in agriculture,
hunting, and fishing is a measure of the extent to which traditional ways have been
retained (Figure 32). Politically, the date of establishment of modern forms of
chiefdom administration, with their developmental budgets and replacement of
many traditional duties and obligations, is a surrogate of modern attitudes (Figure
9). Both are hypothesized to be inversely proportional to migration levels.

Alternative Employment Opportunities

As one of the main causes of migration is assumed to be the search for paid
employment, the presence of such intervening opportunities in the provinces
should either retard the movement of people to the city or redirect the flow. In
Sierra Leone, such alternative sources of employment are represented by the
mines—including diamond, chromite, rutile, and iron. The chromite mines have
now closed and today the iron mines are in the process of reducing their labor
force. The rutile mines are a recent development, so that only proximity to the
diamond areas has been taken as a measure of alternative employment (Figure
32). It is expected that proximity to the diamond fields will have a retarding effect
on the pattern of movement to Freetown.

National Groupings

Many references have been made to intertribal variations in the propensity to
migrate. The fact that the tribal proportions of Freetown do not correspond to

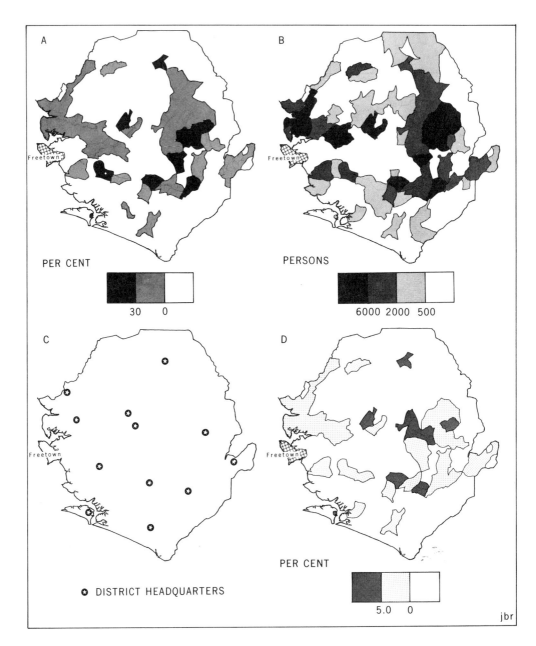

Figure 31.   Explanatory Variables:
A—Percentage of Chiefdom Population Residing in Places of over 2,000 Population; B—Absolute Growth of Urban Places, 1927 to 1963; C—District Headquarters; D—Tertiary Employment

national proportions may suggest that certain tribes do have a higher propensity to migrate (Table 12). The hypothesis was tested by relating the pattern of migration to the pattern of Mende, Temne, and Limba proportions in the population (Figure 33). However, despite the fact that significant statistical associations arise, they

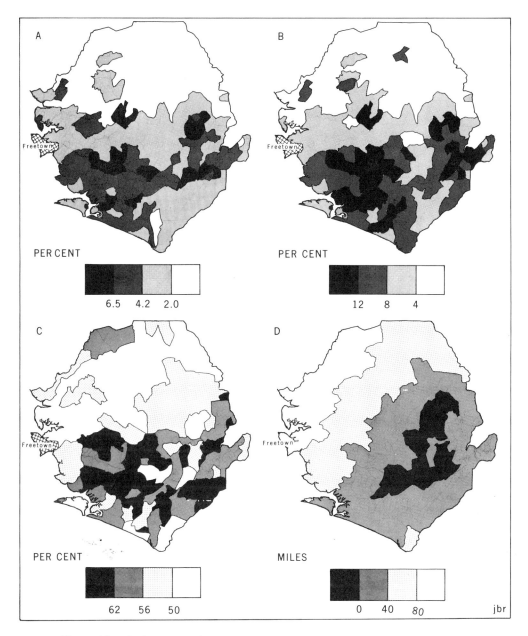

Figure 32.   Explanatory Variables:
A—Literacy in English; B—Percentage of School-Aged Children Attending School; C—Relative Importance of Traditional Sector; D—Distance to Diamond Fields

were considered spurious and were removed from the analysis. Rather than reflect inherent propensities, the relationships indicate the locations of other variables. Tribes in urbanized chiefdoms closer to Freetown do tend to be more mobile, but because of urban living and relative propinquity. The breakdown of the country

114

TABLE 12.   Tribal Composition

	Sierra Leone		Freetown	
	Number	Percentage	Number	Percentage
Creole	41,783	1.92	27,730	21.68
Fulani	66,824	3.06	6,533	5.11
Kissi	48,954	2.25	774	0.58
Kono	104,573	4.80	540	0.42
Kroo	4,793	0.22	4,461	3.49
Kuranko	80,732	3.70	257	0.20
Limba	183,496	8.42	18,410	14.39
Loko	64,459	2.96	5,842	4.57
Mandinko	51,024	2.34	3,141	2.46
Mende	672,831	30.86	12,561	9.82
Sherbro	74,674	3.42	3,051	2.39
Susu	67,288	3.09	3,865	3.02
Temne	648,931	29.76	30,595	23.92
Other	69,933	3.21	10,157	7.94
Total	2,180,355	100.01	127,917	99.99

SOURCE: *1963 Population Census of Sierra Leone,* Vol. II, Table 3.

into north and south regions and the rerunning of the analysis indicated that the tribal variables were statistically important only in areas in which they comprised a minimal proportion of the population. Thus, the association of Mende proportions and rates of migration held only for the north, where there are virtually no Mendes. Similarly, Temnes proved statistically significant only in the south. Hence the tribal-propensities thesis is rejected. The greater movement of some groups reflects merely the action of other variables.

AN ANALYSIS OF THE MOVEMENT TO FREETOWN

The dependent variable, per capita rates of migration, M_i/P_i, was related to each of the set of 15 explanatory variables representing the above hypotheses

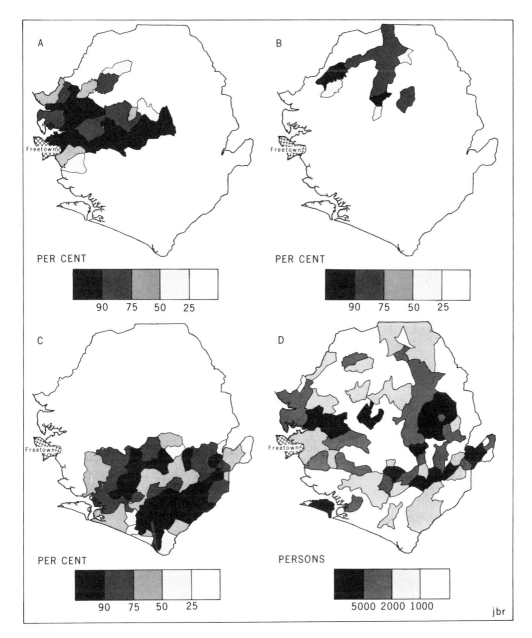

Figure 33.   Explanatory Variables:
          A—Temne Proportions;   B—Limba Proportions;   C—Mende Proportions;
          D—Size of Largest Town

by simple correlation analysis.[24] In one sense the results are disappointing
(Table 13). Although the correlation coefficients all differ statistically from

24. Data were logarithmically transformed to provide linearity. N = 147. Data sources
include archival documents, map measurement, and the recent census.

TABLE 13. SIMPLE CORRELATION COEFFICIENTS

Variable	r
Road Distance	−0.541
Inaccessibility	−0.388
Date Connected	−0.452
Population Density	0.464
Urban Percentage	0.308
Urban Growth	0.291
District Headquarters	0.377
Tertiary Employment	0.338
Date School	−0.248
Literacy	0.267
Education	0.197
Traditional Sector	−0.319
Distance to Diamonds	0.306
Date Native Administration	−0.404
Size of Town	0.383

zero, their association is relatively weak. However, given the complexity of the migration process and the expectation that the influence of certain variables—especially education—will vary regionally, such initial results support all the hypotheses, for the signs are all as predicted. Migration is inversely proportional to distance in its several manifestations, positively associated with the urban, population-density, and education variables and with distance from alternative opportunity, and negatively related to the date of establishment of native administrations and to the strength of the traditional sector.

Movement is the resultant of many factors, which at times operate separately, but most often in combination. Thus, the effects of urban influence on migration are not independent of distance, and the impact of education will partially depend upon the degree of modernization. Hence, the explanatory variables were considered simultaneously in their association with migration. The result is a multiple linear regression of the form

$$Y = \beta_0 + \beta_1 X_1 + \beta_2 X_2 + \ldots + \beta_n X_n$$

TABLE 14. MULTIPLE REGRESSION: ALL VARIABLES

Variable	Regression Coefficient	Standardized Regression Coefficient
Road Distance	−0.411	−1.19
Inaccessibility	−0.324	−1.3?
Date Connected	−12.239	−2.74
Population Density	0.433	2.42
Urban Percentage	−0.026	−0.34
Urban Growth	−0.003	−0.09
District Headquarters	0.491	1.03
Tertiary Employment	0.148	1.10
Date School	−0.841	−0.19
Literacy	−0.068	−0.22
Education	0.430	1.56
Traditional Sector	0.332	0.66
Distance to Diamonds	0.431	4.14
Date Native Administration	−33.685	−0.80
Size of Town	0.219	0.88

where Y represents per capita migration rates; X_1, X_2, . . . , X_n, the explanatory variables; and β_0, β_1, . . . , β_n, the estimating parameters. The regression coefficients, the betas, indicate the extent to which a unit change in each of the explanatory variables is associated with increases or decreases in migration rates (Table 14). The standardized regression coefficients provide a comparative index, indicating the relative strengths of the variables in explaining the variance in migration to Freetown. When all the variables are considered in combination, the degree of explanation is markedly increased from that provided by any one variable alone. All the variables considered jointly account for 60.0 per cent of the variance in migration rates, while distance, the strongest single variable, accounted for only 29.3 per cent. It is apparent that the strongest variables when considered in combination are the distance from the diamond fields, the date at which the area was connected to the transport system, and population density. The other variables are relatively insignificant. However, the expression is complex, and many of the variables are neither statistically nor conceptually independent. The model is of little utility in explaining the migration process.

Some of the shortcomings of the model can be removed by a reduction in the number of variables by a parsimony solution, that is, a successive elimination of the least significant variables until only those which contribute meaningfully to the explanation of the migration process remain (Table 15).

TABLE 15.   MULTIPLE REGRESSION: PARSIMONY SOLUTION

Variable	Regression Coefficient	Standardized Regression Coefficient
Road Distance	−0.848	−4.20
Date Connected	−12.870	−3.05
Population Density	0.450	3.31
Tertiary Employment	0.186	3.21
Education	0.440	3.76
Distance to Diamonds	0.387	5.03

Such a solution effectively reduces the number of explanatory variables (in this case from 15 to 6), and reduces the level of explanation only very slightly to 57.9 per cent. The results indicate that migration is a function of the distance from the diamond fields, the level of education, population density, and the strength of employment levels in the provincial towns and is negatively associated with road distance to Freetown and the date of connection to the transportation system. The relative strengths of the variables, considered in combination, in explaining migration to Freetown can be derived from a comparison of their respective standardized regression coefficients.

The results support the previous contentions on the interaction effects of the variables. Education, when considered separately, was the variable with the lowest association with migration, but in a multiple relationship it becomes one of the more meaningful explanatory factors. Similarly, the explanatory strength of the distance-to-diamonds variable is increased and the strengths of the others are slightly reduced. Conceptually, the expression reduces to four variables—distance, education, population density, and urbanization in the provinces.

Intuitively the model appears plausible, but again the solution is hardly satisfactory. One of the basic underlying requirements of our model is a truly independent set of "independent" variables. Interaction effects are present. Road

TABLE 16.   MATRIX OF FACTOR LOADINGS

Variable	Factor			
	1	2	3	4
Road Distance	−0.11	−0.87	−0.19	0.04
Inaccessibility	0.04	−0.79	−0.21	0.10
Date Connected	−0.29	−0.47	−0.20	0.24
Population Density	0.76	0.16	0.12	−0.00
Urban Percentage	0.83	−0.07	−0.32	−0.12
Urban Growth	0.77	−0.02	−0.33	−0.28
District Headquarters	0.59	0.14	−0.15	0.41
Tertiary Employment	0.89	−0.10	−0.29	−0.08
Date School	−0.31	−0.25	−0.35	−0.37
Literacy	0.68	−0.26	0.53	0.22
Education	0.49	−0.34	0.64	0.28
Traditional Sector	−0.43	−0.34	0.45	−0.47
Distance to Diamonds	−0.34	0.69	−0.27	0.23
Date Native Administration	−0.42	−0.26	−0.52	0.39
Size of Town	0.91	−0.00	−0.21	−0.16
Eigenvalue	5.20	2.58	1.86	1.05
Percentage of variance	34.67	17.20	12.40	7.00

distance is correlated with date connected ($r = 0.358$) and distance to the diamond fields ($r = -0.464$), and is not statistically independent of the other variables. The same is true of the other variables. Thus, despite the fact that (1) the separate effects of each of the variables can be defined, and (2) a combination of variables produces a model of greater descriptive power, a satisfactory representation of the migration process cannot be produced from the combination of the existing varia-

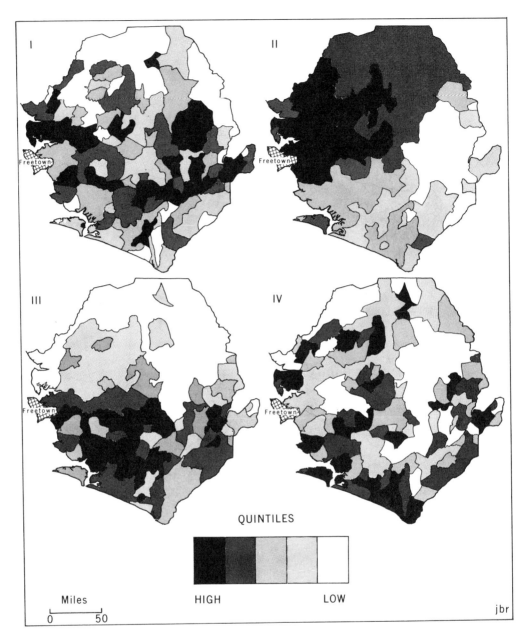

Figure 34. Component Variables

bles. On the one hand, the influence of any one dimension, such as distance effects or urban influences, cannot be expressed by a single index alone, while, on the other hand, the employment of the several measures in combination results in interaction effects which severely weaken the underpinnings of the multiple regression model.

The explanatory variables have much in common. The level of education and literacy rates are not independent, and both are strongly related to the timing of the spread of schools. Yet their covariation with migration is not parallel. Similarly, the several urban measures are interrelated, as are the distance indices. The education measures are not independent of the urban or distance measures, and population density is related to the urban and literacy measures.

However, the set of explanatory variables can be reduced by the method of principal-components analysis, which produces a new and reduced set of *independent* variables expressing the underlying similarities of the original variables (Table 16).

The four independent, orthogonal components together account for 71.28 percent of the variance of the original 15 explanatory variables. A new set of variates results from scoring (or by multiplying the original standardized data matrix by the matrix of factor loadings) and indicates the value of each of the chiefdoms on the four components. This new set of variates contains the underlying generality of the original data in reduced form, and, most important, the new variates are statistically independent.

The first component accounts for about one-third of the variance and is readily recognizable as an urban dimension, although high loadings are also obtained for education, literacy, and population density. The distance variables are virtually excluded and the traditional variable loads negatively, indicating it to be the counterpoint of urban. A mapping of the factor scores indicates the highest values to be associated with the district headquarters, the diamond- and iron-mining areas, and chiefdoms located along the easternmost extension of the railway (Figure 34). Lowest values are associated with the least urban and relatively isolated chiefdoms.

The second component is a linear combination of the distance variables, and its mapping depicts a general pattern of concentric arcs radiating from Freetown. The distortions from a circular pattern depict the deviations from a smooth transport surface. The closer proximity of the north to Freetown is apparent and reflects the historic riverine routes as well as the earlier road connection. The pattern also reflects the isolation of certain chiefdoms and especially the Kono District (Figure 34).

The third factor is essentially an education dimension and forms an areal pattern focused on the southern rivers, where education first took hold in the protectorate. Values generally increase with distance from this core area, with local anomalies being associated with urban areas. The fourth component combines traditional areas with early schools and district headquarters and loads highest on the southern chiefdoms and most of the district headquarters (Figure 34).

Employing the factor scores as a new set of independent variables, a linear descriptive model relating migration to the set of explanatory variables can be derived, having the form

$$Y = \beta_0 + \beta_1 S_1 + \beta_2 S_2 + \beta_3 S_3 + \beta_4 S_4$$

where Y represents per capita rates of migration to Freetown; $\beta_0, \ldots, \beta_4$, the regression coefficients; and $S_1, \ldots, S_4$, the scored factors. The component model removes the interaction effects and permits a realistic interpretation of the parameters.[25] The resultant model takes the form

$$\begin{matrix} [11.90] & [11.05] & [3.16] & [1.72] \\ Y = 1.633 + 0.119S_1 & + 0.221S_2 & + 0.098S_3 & - 0.092S_4 \end{matrix}$$

$$R^2 = 0.630$$

(Note: the figures in brackets are the standardized regression coefficients.)

Hence the component model satisfies the independence requirements of the model and slightly increases the level of explanation from the model employing all of the original variables. It is apparent from an examination of the standardized regression coefficients that the first two components—urbanization and dis-

25. M. G. Kendall, *A Course in Multivariate Statistical Analysis* (New York: Hafner, 1961), pp. 70–74; S. T. Wong, "A Multivariate Statistical Model for Predicting Mean Annual Flood in New England," *Annals of the Association of American Geographers*, LIII (1963), 298–311; G. V. Middleton, "Statistical Studies on Scapolites," *Canadian Journal of Earth Sciences*, I (1964), 23–34.

tance—strongly outweigh the others in the explanation of the pattern of migration.

Since the objective is not to produce the largest possible coefficient of determination but rather to understand and explain the complex migration process, it would be useful to reinterpret the results in terms of the original variables. Such an interpretation is especially important when the components employed in the model fail to yield meaningful real-world interpretation. This is especially vital if the model is to yield policy suggestions.

It will be recalled that the components are linear combinations of the original variables which have been given descriptive names based upon the relative strengths of the factor loadings. Hence the above components-regression model may be written:

$$Y = \beta_0 + \beta_1 \begin{bmatrix} a_{11}X_1 \\ a_{21}X_2 \\ \cdot \\ \cdot \\ \cdot \\ a_{n1}X_n \end{bmatrix} + \beta_2 \begin{bmatrix} a_{12}X_1 \\ a_{22}X_2 \\ \cdot \\ \cdot \\ \cdot \\ a_{n2}X_n \end{bmatrix} + \beta_3 \begin{bmatrix} a_{13}X_1 \\ a_{23}X_2 \\ \cdot \\ \cdot \\ \cdot \\ a_{n3}X_n \end{bmatrix} + \beta_4 \begin{bmatrix} a_{14}X_1 \\ a_{24}X_2 \\ \cdot \\ \cdot \\ \cdot \\ a_{n4}X_n \end{bmatrix}$$

where the a's represent the elements of the matrix of factor loadings, and X_1, . . . , X_n the original variables. By simply collecting terms, the expression can be rewritten:

$$\begin{aligned} Y = \beta_0 &+ (\beta_1 \cdot a_{11} + \beta_2 \cdot a_{12} + \beta_3 \cdot a_{13} + \beta_4 \cdot a_{14})X_1 \\ &+ (\beta_1 \cdot a_{21} + \beta_2 \cdot a_{22} + \beta_3 \cdot a_{23} + \beta_4 \cdot a_{24})X_2 + \ldots \\ &+ (\beta_1 \cdot a_{n1} + \beta_2 \cdot a_{n2} + \beta_3 \cdot a_{n3} + \beta_4 \cdot a_{n4})X_n \end{aligned}$$

which is a predictive linear model describing migration to Freetown in terms of the original variables, while at the same time satisfying the independence assumption of the regression model. The new regression coefficients may be described as reconstituted regression coefficients, or β'.[26]

Expanding the above empirical components regression, the following linear descriptive model is derived:

$$Y = 1.633 - 0.228X_1 - 0.200X_2 - 0.181X_3 + 0.138X_4 + 0.138X_5$$
$$+ 0.063X_6 + 0.081X_7 + 0.063X_8 - 0.093X_9 + 0.055X_{10}$$
$$+ 0.020X_{11} - 0.039X_{12} + 0.063X_{13} - 0.195X_{14} + 0.102X_{15}$$

To compare the relative strengths of the original variables in explaining the migration process, the vector of regression coefficients is standardized. The resultant standardized reconstituted regression coefficients depict the explanatory weights (Table 17).

It is evident that the results are not markedly different from the component-model solution; the distance and urban variables weigh highest and dominate the solution. However, several details are brought to light which were not previously apparent. Certain variables are found to be much more important than

26. In terms of matrices:

Z produces R produces L

where Z is the standardized data matrix, R the correlation matrix, and L the factor-loadings matrix. The factor-score matrix (S) is derived by multiplying the standardized data matrix by the loadings matrix:

$$Z \cdot L = S$$

Employing the scored factors in the predictive model:

$$Y = S \cdot \beta$$

where β is the vector of regression coefficients. Thus,

$$Y = (Z \cdot L) \cdot \beta \quad \text{and} \quad Y = Z \cdot (L \cdot \beta)$$

$L \cdot \beta$ produces the vector of reconstituted regression coefficients (β'), and thus

$$Y = Z \cdot \beta'$$

TABLE 17. STANDARDIZED RECONSTITUTED REGRESSION COEFFICIENTS

Variable	Weight	Variable	Weight
Road Distance	−11.59	Date School	−6.92
Inaccessibility	−9.09	Literacy	6.52
Date Connected	−9.69	Education	3.62
Population Density	11.19	Traditional Sector	−6.64
Urban Percentage	8.30	Distance to Diamonds	2.33
Urban Growth	8.38	Date Native Administration	−10.19
District Headquarters	7.39	Size of Town	10.44
Tertiary Employment	8.71		

the component model would suggest. This is especially true of population density and the date of establishment of Native Administrations. The influence of these variables was submerged within the factors and emerged only by the derivation of the reconstituted regression coefficients.[27] The distance variables all load strongly, and the fact that the date at which an area was connected to the transport system is important lends support to the circular and cumulative theory of information flow and movement. Those places first linked with the city appear to have established and maintained a lasting flow of people to Freetown. There is, in effect, a feedback mechanism, with movement leading to more and better information, which in turn leads to further movement.

Thus, in general terms, levels of urbanization and distance from Freetown are the key dimensions underlying the migration process. The per capita rate of movement to Freetown is inversely proportional to distance from the city, while the strength of the urban dimension indicates that a stepwise migration process is

27. The ordering of explanatory variables as derived from the reconstituted model bears only partial resemblance to those derived by ordinary multiple-regression techniques. Distance to Diamonds is shifted from first to last in relative importance, and the effects of the levels of Education are strongly reduced. At the same time, the Size of Town and Date of Native Administration variables are given added importance. These changes reflect the removal of multicollinearity effects from the multiple-regression model. (After completing this work, I found similar notions in W. F. Massey, "Principal Components Regression in Exploratory Statistical Research," *Journal of the American Statistical Association*, LX [1965], 234–56.)

occurring. In more specific terms, the key variables related to migration rates are road distance to Freetown, population density, the size of the largest urban center in the chiefdom, and the date of establishment of native-administration forms of local government. Several other variables, including measures of urban growth, urban percentage, tertiary employment, relative inaccessibility, date connected to the transport system, and the presence or absence of a district headquarters, are vital, though less important, determinants of the migration pattern. Perhaps as notable is the relative insignificance of the proximity to the diamond fields and the level of education in describing the migration process. The insignificance of the diamonds is likely due to their fairly recent origin as a magnet to population movement, while the relative unimportance of the education variables is due to the fact that the effects of education are strong in the south while weak in the north.[28]

CONCLUSIONS

Migration is a response to the complex set of spatial, social, and economic changes which have characterized much of the modern history of Sierra Leone. People have been spurred to move by the spread of new ideas and opportunities along the expanding transportation system, and their movements have been given a new set of foci by the evolution of a hierarchy of central places. The barrier of distance has been lowered in both a real and a psychological sense. Modern means of transport have made movement less arduous and less costly, while, with the spread of information and the involvement in the money economy, mental images of individual behavior-spaces have markedly expanded.[29] Above all, movement has been a response to the evolving urban system. Solid evidence supports the notion of a

28. For example, the simple correlation coefficient between migration rates and the date of establishment of schools in the south is -0.572, while it is $+0.200$ in the north. Similarly, the coefficients relating migration and literacy for the south and north, respectively, are $+0.622$ and $+0.222$, and for education levels, $+0.533$ and $+0.411$.

29. P. Gould, *On Mental Maps* (Discussion Paper No. 9, Michigan Inter-University Community of Mathematical Geographers, September, 1966).

stepwise process of migration in which the provincial towns act as catalysts, attracting people from the rural areas to the local town, where they acquire new skills, attitudes, and behavior patterns and weaken the ties to the home area and traditional society. Then later, perhaps not until the next generation, many move on to the greater opportunities in the primate city. In effect people seem to be moving up the steps of the urban hierarchy.

Migration is a continuing process, reflecting and indexing the overriding pattern of modernization and change. Its intensity will continue to wax as the rate of progress increases, and it must be recognized as an integral part of the future. The problems it induces will be similar to those experienced in other parts of the world, though perhaps even more intense, as the process of change is telescoped into a much shorter time span and made even more dramatic. The migration process cannot be controlled by government policy or programs other than the strictest imposition of police-state restrictions on movement. Improvements in the rural areas and provincial towns will not stem the flow, but serve to increase it. Migration must be recognized as an increasingly important component of the evolving modernization process and its consequences must be provided for by increased efforts in urban housing, sanitation, food supply, and employment opportunities.

An Overview

Three dominant and tightly interwoven themes have been identified as characterizing the human geography of Sierra Leone during the last seventy years of the colonial period. It is around these themes, which illustrate the spatial dimension of the modernization process, that certain generalizations may be drawn.

A network of rail and road was imposed upon the simple, pre-existing, unimproved mesh of streams and bush paths. The evolution of this system—first as a simple, treelike rail and feeder grid, and then as a more integrated network—was determined largely by the initial location of the rail line. It was only the construction of a wartime road to link the capital with the hinterland as an alternative route that led to the evolution of an independent road system; as the road network gradually surpassed the rail line in areal extent and operating efficiency, the railway lost its magistral importance, fell into decline, and is finally to be abandoned. Geographic space was structured by the emerging transport network as new and very specific avenues of movement were defined. At the same time, the emerging hierarchy of urban places also provided the nexus through which modern elements were spread and within which the new social and economic systems began to evolve. The urban system has been dominated by Freetown, the political capital and point of contact with the wider world, but it also includes at a lower level the towns which have grown up around the colonial administrative centers, the trading points at the junctions in the transport network, and the newer mining-based towns.

Together, the transportation network and the urban hierarchy provide a fabric to the geographic space of Sierra Leone. Not only is the country tied together in each of the administrative, economic, and geographic senses, but the fabric has in large part determined the pattern of diffusion of modernization. The spread of political, social, economic, and institutional change funneled through the transportation network and cascaded down the urban hierarchy. Freetown has always acted as the core area and has dominated the process of modernization, not only in its catalytic role but also by its primacy in terms of physical size and numbers of people and institutions. Freetown has been the focus of government activity, of education, of commerce, industry, and trade, and as such has always held a

129

pre-eminent position on the modernization salient.

In Sierra Leone there is substantial evidence to indicate that the process of modernization and the present status of modernity have the same spatial expression. The strong association of the twenty-two process and status variables on the first modernization component indicate that they have much in common.[1] Naturally there are a few exceptions, such as the relative historical decline of places such as Bonthe and Pujehun, which had many indicators of modernity at the beginning of the twentieth century because of their early trade role. Now these places have declined in a relative sense as trade has been refocused onto the railway axis and the Freetown port, while towns such as Bo, Kenema, Makeni, Lunsar, Koidu, and Yengema have become important provincial urban centers. However, other than the few exceptions, the patterns are remarkably similar and reflect the spatial continuity and recursiveness of the modernization process.

In response to these geographic changes and their resultant behavioral impact, the pattern of internal migration has been given a new focus and orientation. Rural-to-urban movement is now an overriding economic and social phenomenon, and strong evidence exists to support the contention that migration to the city has definite geographic regularity. Rates of movement to Freetown are strongly associated with the urban system and the frictional effects of distance as modified by the transport network. The notion of a stepwise movement of peoples upward through the urban hierarchy is supported. Any general migration model for underdeveloped areas undergoing rapid urbanization would be dominated by movements from the rural areas to the growing provincial towns, and then from these towns to the large metropolitan centers. The provincial towns act as catalysts to movement from rural areas to the large cities rather than as alternatives.

The process of change in Sierra Leone is dominated to an amazing degree by spatial order and pattern. Modernization is a geographic phenomenon with obvious spatial expression; its pattern of spread is not a simple contagious process, but is strongly influenced and determined by the transport network and the urban-administrative hierarchy. Similarly, migration is in large part conditioned by the

1. See Table 9, p. 90.

same elements of the spatial fabric. Thus the human geography of the country provides the framework for change. Cultural and ethnic patterns within the population are very real and do influence alterations, but the over-all pattern of change in the country is a function of its geography—the spatial organization of the countryside by network and hierarchy. The spatial dimension affords the key focus toward understanding the phenomenon of modernization.

Bibliography

BOOKS AND ARTICLES

Alldridge, T. J. *The Sherbro and Its Hinterland*. London: Macmillan, 1901.
_____. *A Transformed Colony: Sierra Leone as It Was, and as It Is: Its Progress, Peoples, Native Customs and Undeveloped Wealth*. London: Seeley, 1910
Bagai, O. P. "A Statistical Study of Exports of Sierra Leone, 1920–64." Mimeo. Freetown: University College of Sierra Leone, 1965.
Baker, E. D. "The Development of Secondary Education in Sierra Leone." Ph.D. dissertation, University of Michigan, 1963.
Balandier, G. "The Colonial Situation." In *Africa: Social Problems of Change and Conflict*, ed. P. L. van den Berghe, pp. 36–57. San Francisco: Chandler, 1965.
Banton, M. "Tribal Headmen in Freetown." *Journal of African Administration*, VI (1954), 140–44.
_____. *West African City*. London: Oxford University Press, 1957.
Beals, R. E., Levy, M. B., Menezes, C. F., and Moses, L. N. *Labor Migration and Regional Development in Ghana*. Report of the Transportation Center, Northwestern University, January, 1966.
Berry, B. J. L. "City Size Distribution and Economic Development." *Economic Development and Cultural Change*, IX (1961), 573–88.
Best, J. R. "A History of the Sierra Leone Railway, 1899–1949." Mimeo. Freetown, 1949.
Black, C. E. *The Dynamics of Modernization*. New York: Harper & Row, 1967.
Breese, G. *Urbanization in Newly Developing Countries*. Englewood Cliffs, N.J.: Prentice-Hall, 1966.
Cardew, Governor F. *Railway Schemes for the Colony of Sierra Leone*. Address presented to the Liverpool Chamber of Commerce, August 1, 1895; published in pamphlet form by the African Trade Section of the Incorporated Chamber of Commerce of Liverpool, August 1895.
Cary, Joyce. *Britain and West Africa*. London: Longmans, Green, 1946.
Chorley, R. J. and Haggett, P. "Trend Surface Mapping in Geographic Research." *Transactions of the Institute of British Geographers*, XXXVII (1965), 47–67.
Christaller, W. *Central Places in Southern Germany*, trans. C. W. Baskin. Englewood Cliffs, N.J.: Prentice-Hall, 1966.
Church, R. J. "The Railways of West Africa—A Geographical and Historical Analysis." Ph.D. dissertation, University of London, 1943.
Clarke, J. I. *Sierra Leone in Maps*. London: University of London Press, 1966.

Cox-George, N. A. *Finance and Development in West Africa: The Sierra Leone Experi-ence.* London: Dobson, 1961.

Crowder, M. *West Africa under Colonial Rule.* London: Hutchinson; Evanston, Ill.: Northwestern University Press, 1968.

Davies, E. "Roads and Road Transport in Sierra Leone." Mimeo. Freetown, n.d.

Eisenstadt, S. N. *Modernization: Protest and Change.* Englewood Cliffs, N.J.: Prentice-Hall, 1966.

Fyfe, C. H. "European and Creole Influence in the Hinterland of Sierra Leone before 1896." *Sierra Leone Studies,* VI (1956), 113–23.

_____. *A History of Sierra Leone.* London: Oxford University Press, 1962.

_____. *Sierra Leone Inheritance.* London: Oxford University Press, 1964.

Fyfe, C. H. and Jones, E., eds. *Freetown: A Symposium.* Freetown: Sierra Leone University Press, 1968.

Goddard, T. N. *The Handbook of Sierra Leone.* London: Grant Richards, 1925.

Gould. P. "Data, Decisions and Development in Transportation: Some Lessons from the East African Experience." Mimeo. University Park, Pa., 1965.

_____. "A Note on Research into the Diffusion of Development." *Journal of Modern African Studies,* II (1964), 123–25.

_____. "On the Geographic Interpretation of Eigenvalues." *Transactions of the Institute of British Geographers,* XLII (1967), 53–86.

_____. *On Mental Maps.* Discussion Paper No. 9, Michigan Inter-University Community of Mathematical Geographers, September 1966.

_____. *Transportation in Ghana.* Evanston, Ill.: Northwestern University Studies in Geography, No. 5, 1960.

Gregory, S. *Rainfall over Sierra Leone.* University of Liverpool, Department of Geography, Research Paper No. 2, 1965.

Hagerstrand, T. "Migration and Area." *Lund Studies in Geography,* Series B, XIII (1957), 27–158.

_____. "The Propagation of Innovation Waves." *Lund Studies in Geography,* Series B, IV (1952).

Hailey, Lord. *An African Survey: Revised 1956.* London: Oxford University Press, 1957.

_____. *Native Administration in the British African Territories: Part III, West Africa,* pp. 281–328. London: H.M.S.O., 1951.

_____. *Native Administration in the British African Territories: Part IV, A General Survey of the System of Native Administration.* London: H.M.S.O., 1951.

Hancock, W. K. *Survey of British Commonwealth Affairs.* Vol. III: *Problems of Eco-*

nomic Policy 1918–1939, Part II. London: Oxford University Press, 1942.

Hargreaves, J. D. "The Establishment of the Sierra Leone Protectorate and the Insurrection of 1898." *Cambridge Historical Journal,* XII (1956), 56–80.

Harvey, M. E. E. "A Geographical Study of the Pattern, Processes and Consequences of Urban Growth in Sierra Leone in the Twentieth Century." Ph.D. dissertation, University of Durham, 1966.

Hedges, D. M. "Progress of Kambia District Council, Sierra Leone." *Journal of African Administration,* V (1953), 30–34.

Herskovits, M. J. "Special Problems in Underdeveloped Countries: Discussion." *American Economic Review,* XLIV (1959), 200.

Hicks, U. K. *Development from Below.* London: Oxford University Press, 1961.

Howard, A. "The Role of Freetown in the Commercial Life of Sierra Leone." In *Freetown: A Symposium,* ed. C. H. Fyfe and E. Jones, pp. 38–64.

Institute for Planning and Development Ltd. *Sierra Leone: National Urbanization Plan.* Israel: Institute for Planning and Development Ltd., December 1965.

Italconsult (United Nations Development Program Special Fund, Executing Agency, International Bank for Reconstruction and Development). *Land Transport Study, Sierra Leone Railway: Interim Report.* Rome: Italconsult, December 1966.

————. *Land Transport Survey: 10-Year Investment Programme (Interim Report).* Rome: Italconsult, June 1967.

Jefferson, M. "The Law of Primate Cities." *Geographical Review,* XXIX (1939), 226–32.

Kamarck, A. M. *The Economics of African Development.* New York: Praeger, 1967.

Kendall, M. G. *A Course in Multivariate Statistical Analysis.* New York: Hafner, 1961.

Kilson, M. *Political Change in a West African State: A Study of the Modernization Process in Sierra Leone.* Cambridge: Harvard University Press, 1966.

Kuper, H., ed. *Urbanization and Migration in West Africa.* Berkeley: University of California Press, 1965.

Laan, H. L. van der. *The Sierra Leone Diamonds: An Economic Study Covering the Years 1952–1961.* London: Oxford University Press, 1965.

Lewis, R. *Sierra Leone: A Modern Portrait.* London: H.M.S.O., 1954.

Little, K. *The Mende of Sierra Leone.* London: Routledge & Kegan Paul, 1967.

————. *West African Urbanization.* Cambridge: Cambridge University Press, 1965.

Lloyd, P. C. *Africa in Social Change.* London: Penguin Books, 1967.

Lystad, R. A., ed. *The African World: A Survey of Social Research.* New York: Praeger, 1965.

Meinig, D. W. *On the Margins of the Good Earth.* Chicago: Rand McNally, 1962.

Middleton, G. V. "Statistical Studies on Scapolites." *Canadian Journal of Earth Sciences*, I (1964), 23–34.

Mitchell, P. K. "Trade Routes of the Early Sierra Leone Protectorate." *Sierra Leone Studies*, XVI (1962), 204–17.

Morrill, R. L. "Waves of Spatial Diffusion." *Journal of Regional Science*, VIII (1968), 1–18.

O'Donovan, P. "When the Empire Closed Down." *The Observer* (London), January 21, 1968, p. 2.

Olsson, G. "Distance and Human Interaction: A Migration Study." *Geografiska Annaler*, Series B, XLVII (1965), 3–43.

————. *Distance and Human Interaction: A Review and Bibliography*. Philadelphia: Regional Science Research Institute, 1965.

Owen, W. *Strategy for Mobility*. Washington, D.C.: Brookings Institution, 1964.

Porter, A. T. *Creoledom*. London: Oxford University Press, 1963.

Pratt, S. A. J. "The Development of the Sierra Leone Railway: Vol. I—The Existing System." Mimeo. Freetown, 1966.

Ravenstein, E. G. "The Laws of Migration." *Journal of the Royal Statistical Society*, XLVIII (1885), 167–227; LII (1889), 241–301.

Reilly, W. J. "Methods for the Study of Retail Relationships." *University of Texas Bulletin*, No. 2944, 1929.

Riddell, J. B. "Toward an Understanding of the Friction of Distance." M.A. thesis, University of Toronto, 1965.

Saylor, R. G. "The Economic System of Sierra Leone with Special Reference to the Role of Government." Ph.D. dissertation, Duke University, 1966.

Shelford, F. "The Development of West Africa by Railways." Paper read before the Royal Colonial Institute, April 12, 1904.

————. "Some Features of the West African Government Railways." Paper read before the Institute of Civil Engineers, 1912.

Simms, R. P. *Urbanization in West Africa: A Review of Current Literature*. Evanston, Ill.: Northwestern University Press, 1965.

Soja, E. *The Geography of Modernization in Kenya*. Syracuse: Syracuse University Press, 1968.

Stewart, J. Q. "The Development of Social Physics." *American Journal of Physics*, XVIII (1950), 239–53.

_____. "A Measure of the Influence of a Population at a Distance." *Sociometry*, V (1952), 63–71.

Stouffer, S. A. "Intervening Opportunities: A Theory Relating Mobility and Distance." *American Sociological Review*, V (1940), 845–67.

Sumner, D. L. *Education in Sierra Leone*. Freetown: Government Printer, 1963.

Taaffe, E. J., Morrill, R. L., and Gould, P. R. "Transportation Expansion in Underdeveloped Countries: A Comparative Analysis." *Geographical Review*, LIII (1963), 503–29.

Transportation Consultants Inc. *Transport Survey of Sierra Leone*. Washington, D.C.: Transportation Consultants Inc., 1963.

Weiner, M., ed. *Modernization: The Dynamics of Growth*. New York: Basic Books, 1966.

Williams, G. J. "A Relative Relief Map of Sierra Leone. *Sierra Leone Geographical Journal*, XI (1967), 11–14.

Wong, S. T. "A Multivariate Statistical Model for Predicting Mean Annual Flood in New England," *Annals of the Association of American Geographers*, LIII (1963), 298–311.

Zipf, G. K. *Human Behavior and the Principle of Least Effort*. Reading, Mass.: Addison-Wesley, 1949.

GOVERNMENT DOCUMENTS

Great Britain

Colonial Development and Welfare Acts: Return of Schemes. Annual papers from 1942 to present.

Colonial Office. *Colonial Reports, Annual, Sierra Leone*. 1891–1958.

_____. *Despatch Book (Governors of Sierra Leone to the Colonial Office)*. 1901–1936. Public Records Office.

_____. *Report by the Hon. W. G. A. Ormsby-Gore, M. P. (Parliamentary Under-Secretary of State for the Colonies), on His Visit to West Africa during the Year 1926*.

Hammond, F. D. *Report on the Sierra Leone Government Railway*. London: The Crown Agents for the Colonies, 1922.

Parliamentary Papers. Papers Relating to the Construction of Railways in Sierra Leone, Lagos and the Gold Coast. Parliamentary Paper 1905 Cd2325 lvi 361.

Sierra Leone

(All published in Freetown by the Government Printer.)

Annual Report on the Administration of the Provinces. 1927–55.
Blue Book. 1897–1939.
Blyden, E. W. *Report on the Falaba Expedition, 1872.* 1872.
Bunning, A. J. F. "Report on a Visit to Sierra Leone by A. J. F. Bunning, Adviser on Inland Transport to the Secretary of State for the Colonies." Mimeo. 1949.
Carney, D. *Ten Year Plan of Economic and Social Development for Sierra Leone: 1962/63–1971/72.* 1962.
Central Statistics Office. *1963 Population Census of Sierra Leone.* 1965.
Co-operative Department. *Annual Report of the Co-operative Department.* 1948–57.
———. *District Development Plans.* 1949.
Davidson, H. W. *Report on the Functions and Finances of District Councils in Sierra Leone.* 1953.
Development Estimates. 1960/61–1966/67.
Development Plan of the Health Care Services of Sierra Leone. 1962.
The Development Programme in Education for Sierra Leone, 1964–1970. 1964.
Education Department. *Annual Report of the Education Department.* 1914–63.
———. "Statistics of Schools in the Protectorate, 1955." Mimeo. 1955.
———. *Triennial Survey 1955–57.* 1958.
The First Year: A Progress Report on the Ten-Year Plan. 1963.
Jack, D. T. *Economic Survey of Sierra Leone.* 1958.
Juxon-Smith, Col. A. T. *Statement on the Budget for 1967/68.* 1967.
Kesson, J. M. "Report on Sierra Leone Railways." Mimeo. 1965.
Legislative Council Debates. 1922–63.
Medical Department. *Annual Report of the Medical Department.* 1900–1959.
Nicholls, E. H. D. *Report on the Administration of the Public Works Department, Sierra Leone.* 1928.
An Outline of the Ten-Year Plan for the Development of Sierra Leone. 1946.
A Plan of Economic Development for Sierra Leone. 1949.
Post Office Department. *Annual Report of the Post Office Department.* 1918–1962/63.
———. *Annual Report of the Post Office Savings Bank.* 1961–62.

Progress Report on the Development Programme. 1946–51.

A Progress Report on Economic and Social Development, April 27, 1961–March 31, 1965. 1965.

Protectorate Handbook. 1947–62.

Public Works Department. *Annual Report of the Public Works Department.* 1919–1962/63.

Railway Department. *Annual Report of the Railway Department.* 1909–1961/62.

Report of the Co-operative Mission to Sierra Leone. 1950.

Report on Co-operation in Sierra Leone. 1949.

Sessional Papers. *Report of the Committee Appointed to Enquire into the Medical Needs of the Towns and Villages of the Peninsula, Outside Freetown.* No. 6, 1923.

———. *Despatches Relating to the Surplus Balances Development Program, 1925.* No. 15, 1925.

———. *Supplementary Programme of Motor Road Construction.* No. 5, 1927.

———. *Despatches and Correspondence Relating to Pioneer Roads.* No. 3, 1928.

———. *Despatches Relating to the Programme of Motor Road Construction in the Protectorate for the Years 1929 to 1931.* No. 6, 1928.

———. *Administrative Sub-divisions of the Colony and the Protectorate.* No. 4, 1930.

———. *Report by Mr. J. S. Fenton, O.B.E., District Commissioner, on a Visit to Nigeria and on the Application of the Principles of Native Administration to the Protectorate of Sierra Leone.* No. 3, 1935.

———. *Education Policy in the Protectorate.* No. 5, 1937.

———. *Correspondence Relating to the Reorganization of Protectorate Administration.* No. 5, 1939.

———. *Administrative Reorganization of the Protectorate.* No. 7, 1945.

———. *Report on the Development of Education in Sierra Leone.* No. 11, 1948.

Sierra Leone Gazette. Weekly, 1904–67.

Ministry of Transport and Communications. "Project for the Improvement of the Sierra Leone Railway." Mimeo. 1964.

Department of Works, Highway Division. "Paper on the Italconsult Study." Mimeo. 1967.

Index